"Warm, inviting, and helpful, this gem of a book brings mindfulness down to earth for adolescents and young adults. Gina Biegel is a world-class expert on this subject, and she writes straight from her own heart, offering simple and powerful ideas and practices. Teens are under more pressure than ever these days, and this book is a wonderful resource."

—**Rick Hanson, PhD**, author of *Buddha's Brain*

"I have found the benefits of mindfulness to be indispensable in my personal and professional life. I only wish I had known about this practice when I was younger. Gina Biegel's book serves as an excellent resource for young folks looking to integrate this transformative practice into their own lives. With peer pressure, information overload, and constant connection to social media an ever present reality, I would recommend it to any student."

—**Tim Ryan**, congressman and author of *A Mindful Nation*

"Gina Biegel's book is a must-have for all adolescents. From her letter to teens in the beginning addressing social media, to the engaging activities throughout the book, teenagers will recognize their own personal issues and begin to understand that they aren't alone. The activities are accessible and the explanations easy to understand. These activities, many of which are new in this second edition, provide adolescents with a myriad of tools to address teen stressors, problems, and angst. I can imagine this becoming teens' favorite 'go-to' book, as it provides much needed relief. I wish it had been around when I was a teen, and I really wish I had had this tool when my own children were teenagers. I heartily endorse Biegel's book and I encourage you to give it to every teen you know!"

—**Laurie Grossman**, director of program development and outreach at Inner Explorer, cofounder of Mindful Schools, and coauthor of *Master of Mindfulness*

"In the updated edition of her popular stress reduction workbook, Gina Biegel offers teens a set of practical and powerful tools to help them recognize their problems and resolve them in a healthy way."

—**Susan Kaiser Greenland**, author of *Mindful Games* and *The Mindful Child*

"As a mindfulness researcher and the mom of a teen, I am so glad that Gina Biegel has penned this workbook. It's accessible, user-friendly, and offers mindfulness training in a manner that resonates with teens. As he or she works through this book, you will see your teen transform from stressed out and distracted to attentive and self-aware. A must-have for every adolescent's wellness toolkit!"

—**Amishi Jha, PhD**, University of Miami

"Gina Biegel's *The Stress Reduction Workbook for Teens* is *the* go-to book for teens wanting to lower their stress and navigate the challenges of life with more skill and resilience. Written in a way that is very accessible and relevant to teens, the book empowers teens to access inner resources to manage difficult situations and make wise choices. An excellent resource for teens and those who care about them."

—**Lidia Zylowska, MD**, associate professor in the department of psychiatry at the University of Minnesota, founding member of the University of California, Los Angeles' Mindful Awareness Research Center, and author of *The Mindfulness Prescription for Adult ADHD*

"This is a useful workbook for teens. It draws on and distills decades of experience and research on mindfulness and self-regulation, and shows teens how to do it!"

—**Trudy Goodman, PhD**, founding teacher at insightLA.org

"In *The Stress Reduction Workbook for Teens*, Gina Biegel offers a dynamic and engaging resource for adolescents struggling with stress—and what teen isn't struggling with stress these days? This book has the potential to empower young adults to find healthy relationships with their bodies, hearts, minds, and their relationships with others. Gina writes from her many years of expertise as a researcher and mindfulness practitioner."

—**Daniel Rechtschaffen, MFT**, author of *The Way of Mindful Education* and *The Mindful Education Workbook*

"Gina Biegel offers us key tools for teens to bring mindfulness into their lives in order to manage everyday stressors, reduce self-harm, and increase their toolkit of positive coping strategies. I find this book to be accessible to all teens!"

—**Elisha Goldstein, PhD**, author of *Uncovering Happiness*, and coauthor of *MBSR Every Day*

"A gift for our stressed-out teens and the grown-ups who work with (or live with) them!"

—**Christopher Willard, PsyD**, author of *Mindfulness for Teen Anxiety* and coauthor of *Mindfulness for Teen Depression*; Cambridge Health Alliance/ Harvard Medical School

"Bringing mindfulness to teens is a noble mission, particularly when it includes not only the practice of mindfulness but also connecting teens to a better understanding of their thoughts, feelings, and emotions. It's a much-needed workbook and an empowering way to encourage reflection, self-discovery, and personal change."

—**Theo Koffler**, author, educator, and founder of Mindfulness Without Borders

"If you know a teenager, you probably know someone who gets stressed. With hormones raging through their bodies and extra sensitivity, teens feel things intensely. Their thoughts and feelings can produce confusion, lack of confidence, and unpredictable behavior. However, with increased awareness, all that passion can produce amazing results born of penetrating wisdom and deep caring. Gina Biegel's *The Stress Reduction Workbook for Teens* is a perfect guidebook to help a teen center themselves and access the wisdom and love right inside. This is an excellent offering of practices that, when applied, can make a real difference in any teen's life."

—**James Baraz**, coauthor of *Awakening Joy*, and cofounding teacher of Spirit Rock Meditation Center

"As a parent of two teens, and someone who works with people who are often burdened by too much stress, this workbook is a tremendous resource. The information and activities contained within offer very practical and tactical solutions to so many of the challenges and stressors facing our teen population, and for the parents of and professionals who work with those teens. Gina Beigel's workbook is like a soothing, warm towel that offers much relief and relaxation for an achy and stressed mind and body."

—**Todd H. Corbin, CPC**, is a stress expert, mindfulness teacher, professional speaker, and coach

"*The Stress Reduction Workbook for Teens* is a practical and useful resource for teens. The accessible and clear activities introduce young people to mindfulness in ways that are relevant to their lives—practices they can put to use right away. Through the guided personal reflections, young people will better understand their stresses and coping mechanisms, for good or for bad, and learn how to shift their behaviors to more helpful responses with mindfulness."

> —**Jessica Morey, MA**, executive director of Inward Bound Mindfulness Education

"Not only is the workbook an excellent resource for teens in being with the stress of everyday life, it also provides a wealth of strategies that can be used in all aspects of their lives to promote positive health and well-being using the well-documented techniques of mindfulness. In our teaching of teens in high schools, we have shared activities that help teens identify stressors in their lives, strengthen self-awareness, and develop the ability to choose how to respond. I would highly recommend it to be part of any high school's resource library."

> —**Heidi Bornstein**, founder of Mindfulness Everyday

"Gina Biegel offers a practical and easy to use, yet comprehensive and thoughtful workbook in *The Stress Reduction Workbook for Teens*. I wish I had had such an insightful resource during my own adolescence, and will be sure to share it with my own daughter."

> —**Jennifer Cohen Harper, MA, E-RCYT**, founder of Little Flower Yoga and the School Yoga Project, author of *Little Flower Yoga for Kids*, and mom

"This workbook is a gift for teens. It offers both mindfulness instruction and stress reduction techniques in a language teens will relate to. The thoughtful exercises and clear instruction are sure to help teens navigate their turbulent years with wisdom and self-compassion."

> —**Diana Winston**, director of mindfulness education at UCLA's Mindful Awareness Research Center, author of *Wide Awake*, and coauthor of *Fully Present*

the stress reduction workbook for teens

SECOND EDITION

mindfulness skills to help you deal with stress

GINA M. BIEGEL, MA, LMFT

Instant Help Books
An Imprint of New Harbinger Publications, Inc.

Publisher's Note

This publication is designed to provide accurate and authoritative information in regard to the subject matter covered. It is sold with the understanding that the publisher is not engaged in rendering psychological, financial, legal, or other professional services. If expert assistance or counseling is needed, the services of a competent professional should be sought.

Distributed in Canada by Raincoast Books

Copyright © 2017 by Gina M. Biegel
        Instant Help Books
        An imprint of New Harbinger Publications, Inc.
        5674 Shattuck Avenue
        Oakland, CA 94609
        www.newharbinger.com

Rumi, excerpt from "The Guesthouse," translated by Coleman Barks. Copyright © 1997 by Coleman Barks. Used by permission.

Cover design by Amy Shoup

Acquired by Jess O'Brien

Edited by Karen Schaeder

Library of Congress Cataloging-in-Publication Data on file

19   18   17

10   9   8   7   6   5   4   3   2   1   First Printing

To all teens who suffer and learn to persevere in life: I hope this book provides one of the many steps for you on your journey to discovery, insight, growth, and change.

I take a deep bow to the teens who are suffering or who have suffered in silence and guide us from beyond. Specifically, to the O'Sullivan family, as Tomas lights the way for all of us.

I am humbled and honored to do the work that I do.

Mindful blessings,

Gina Biegel

contents

Dear Teens,

I am a therapist who specializes in working with people your age. When I was a teen, there was no texting, Facebook, Instagram, tablets, or iPhones. The Internet had just come out, and phones were plugged into walls or in booths. We also had the luxury of something you don't have today—anonymity. While being a teen was difficult *even then*, I can only imagine how much more complex it is for you today!

I have worked with thousands of teens, helping them navigate their way through this challenging period of life. I've helped teens manage and deal with experiences they never thought they could get through, deal with, or face.

What is common to all of these teens?

They are suffering! They have pain! They are stressed!

While everyone's reasons may be different, all teens know what you mean when you talk about suffering, pain, and stress. Dealing with the stress of being a teen can be beyond difficult—just know you are not alone in experiencing it. Often people are stressed and don't really know it or see what they can do about it. Some even react to stress in ways that are harmful.

I've written this book to guide you to other ways. It is intended to help you manage suffering, pain, and stress with *mindfulness*. Through working on the activities in this book, you will be able to

- *notice* emotions, rather than *hide* or *suppress* them;

- learn how to *respond* rather than *react*;

- have *power* in situations where you feel *powerless*;

- start *being* and *living* rather than merely *existing*;

- *control* your actions and *own* your *decisions*.

The best way to use this book is to work through the activities from start to finish, because each activity builds on the ones that precede it. You'll also find a host of materials for download at the website for this book: http://www.newharbinger. com/40187. At the end of the book, there are details about how to access these materials.

If you come to an activity that doesn't fit, you can move on, but I encourage you to try it first. If it's uncomfortable, try it again. A number of the activities are mindfulness-based practices that you can use over and over again. Consider making a daily practice of the ones you like most.

If you're like many people, you find it easy to look at the negatives in your life and the qualities you don't like so much about yourself. This book is about building on resources, skills, and positive qualities you might not even realize you have. Through its activities, you can move from "poor me" thinking to "I can get through this!" thinking. After you work through the activities, you will have a wide range of tools to help you manage pain and stress so you can live the life you want.

This book is not meant to take the place of counseling. Working through some of these activities might bring up painful emotions or memories that require the support of a mental health professional. Please talk with a mental health professional or an adult you trust to discuss these issues further.

I know it takes strength and courage to change, and I applaud you for taking the first and most important steps. The work you do will help you better understand your suffering, pain, and stress and give you new tools for healing, being, and living.

Warmly,

Gina Biegel

letter to parents and professionals

Dear Parents and Professionals,

Life today is challenging, especially for teens. Parenting in a world of social media is hard work. Raising teens in our fast-paced and technologically advanced society is a complex job. Thank you for picking up and looking through this book. I understand that in doing so, you likely know a teen, are the parent of a teen, or are working with a teen who is struggling. You may be searching for resources and guidance. Or you may be trying to learn new ways to best support teens in doing the courageous and difficult work of healing from; learning about; and managing their stress, emotions, and behaviors. My professional and lived experiences with teens have guided my practical work and led me to write as a way of helping others. I am grateful that you have begun this process. Your support, love, and compassion for teens are essential gifts!

In my professional journey, I have drawn from different theories and approaches, created and used a range of tools and resources, and adapted and refined my practices to better fit the needs of those I work with. In my fifteen years of practice working with individual teens and their families, and in groups, I have listened, observed, experimented, and learned. I have also been present with those in my care, finding them to be my best teachers and guides. With them, I have learned how important it is to create a safe and trusting environment for vulnerability and exploration and to work together as a supportive treatment team.

My intention is that the activities in this workbook and the supplementary materials available at http://www.newharbinger.com/40187 be applicable and accessible to teens and their families. These are tools that teens, parents, and practitioners can add to their toolkits for healing, being, and living.

There is flexibility in how you approach this workbook. You can start from beginning to end or do what feels right and use the specific activity that stands out to you or seems like a best fit for the teen. The only caveat is that the mindfulness-based practices do build upon one another. It is like building a muscle. You would want to start with a lighter weight and build up to a heavier weight; similarly, you want to build a muscle of mindfulness. It is recommended to start with the shorter, more guided mindfulness practices earlier in this book and work your way to the longer, less guided practices.

The beginning activities (activities 1–6) allow for teens' exploration and understanding of stress and the role stress and stressors have in life. Activities 7–35, the majority of the workbook, are mindfulness based. I view mindfulness as a solution to combating the mental and physical health difficulties of teens today. The mindfulness activities unfold in three parts:

- activities that allow for foundational mindfulness development

- activities that focus on building social skills, communication, and relationship development

- activities that are intended to improve emotion regulation and metacognition.

I am honored to be able to work alongside you throughout this healing journey.

With gratitude,

Gina Biegel, MA, LMFT

letting go of your problems   1

The first step to manage and work through your problems is to identify what your problems actually are. One way to identify your problems is to reflect on these two questions:

What do you want to be different in your life right now?

What is going on in your life right now that isn't working for you and is possibly a problem?

There is space to answer these questions below, but first consider the following:

- Write what is real and true for you, not what someone else would want you to write.

- Write whatever comes to your mind. What you write here is for you. If you would feel safer, write it on a separate piece of paper.

- After you have written everything you can think of, take an extra minute or two and see if anything else arises for you. Maybe there is something lingering and long-standing that you kind of pushed to the side in your mind but is still a problem in your life.

What do *you* want to be different in your life right now?

What is going on in your life right now that isn't working for you and is possibly a problem?

Write your notes here:

_____

_____

_____

_____

_____

_____

_____

mindful takeaway   Now that you have identified and written your problems down on paper, you don't have to hold them inside anymore. Take a picture of this page, and keep it in a safe personal place so that you can always go back to this list if and when you need to. When you've completed this workbook, look back at your answers to these questions.

something more

Letting Go of Your Problems

When it comes to working on the activities in this book, you do not need to have your problems constantly on your mind. You already have to deal with some or all of them in your day-to-day life. You don't need to hold on to them; they can stay here. Feel free to let go of your problems while you work on the activities in this book.

What do you think of the idea of letting go of your problems and leaving them here?

_____

_____

_____

Is this something you can try? If so, how?

_____

_____

_____

Goal Attainment and Non-Striving

Working on the activities in this book, you do not have to strive to accomplish any goal or get a particular outcome. Just begin these activities with an open mind and the thought that you might learn something new, interesting, and helpful. In almost every aspect of your life, you do something to accomplish a goal or outcome. In this situation, do the opposite.

What is it like for you to consider non-striving as you try to reduce your problems?

_____

_____

_____

Have there been other times in your life when you wished you didn't have to strive to accomplish something? Tell about one of these times.

_____

_____

_____

_____

_____

defining and understanding stress 2

When people say they are stressed out, you generally know what they mean, but we all actually define and experience stress differently. Some people explain it as an uncomfortable emotion, some refer to physical sensations, and some focus on how it affects their thinking.

Stress is *universal* in that everyone has some understanding about what it means to be stressed, but stress is also *individual* in that how each person experiences stress is vastly different. Look at how Aidan and Lindsey define stress.

> *Aidan defines stress as a sharp pain in his chest, in his head, and way too much pressure from other people.*

✱ ✱ ✱

> *Lindsey defines stress as feeling overwhelmed, worrying, and being overloaded with things to do.*

Here are some words people use to define stress in *emotional* terms:

apprehensive	worried
overwhelmed	frustrated
depressed	freaking out
unhappy	lost or confused
nervous	overcommitted
anxious	out of control
uncomfortable	wound up
angry	stretched too thin

Here are some words people use to define stress in *physical* terms:

tension	stomachaches
panic	dizziness
aches and pains	excessive appetite
chest pains	decreased appetite or no appetite
headaches	feeling light-headed or faint
jitteriness	fidgety
trouble breathing	restless
trouble sleeping	unable to sit still

And people might use these words to define stress in terms of their *thoughts*:

overthinking	going over things repeatedly
being in a negative state of mind	having bad thoughts
being unable to focus on anything else	exaggerating things
not being able to concentrate	having too much to think about
blanking out on things	having trouble thinking
constantly thinking about something	having too many things to do

On the categories above, mark any of these terms you have used to define stress. Write the ones you marked here.

_____

_____

_____

Which category best applies to the way you describe stress: emotional terms, physical terms, or in your thoughts?

_____

What other words or ways have you used to define stress that are not listed above?

_____

_____

What is your definition of stress or being stressed out?

_____

_____

_____

something more

When in your day-to-day life you find yourself using the words you just listed, it is a red flag that you are stressed. Considering your current stress level, answer these questions:

How is stress playing a part in your life right now?

_____

_____

_____

Do you want the amount of stress in your life to change?

_____

_____

Which people, places, situations, or other things in your life are stressful to you right now?

_____

_____

_____

Which of these things can you actually change?

_____

_____

_____

life stressors: what is stressing you out? 3

Something that causes you stress is called a *stressor*. Finding out what your stressors are is an important first step toward change and in possibly finding some relief.

Marti works ten hours a week in addition to being in a musical at school and taking a few honors classes. She doesn't know how she'll be able to manage it all. By the time she gets home from either work or rehearsal, it is nine o'clock, and she still has three hours of homework to do. To make things even worse, her friends are mad because she isn't spending a lot of time with them.

✳ ✳ ✳

Nathan is upset because his best friend and his girlfriend want him to choose between them. He would like to be able to hang out with both of them together, but when he is with one, he doesn't feel free to include the other. On top of this, his parents are going through a divorce. Nathan also has a lot of trouble with many of his courses, and his father puts a lot of pressure on him to do better in school.

You probably find it easy to see why Marti and Nathan feel stressed. Do you know what your stressors are right now? Circle all that apply to you.

With your friends

peer pressure (sex/drinking/drugs)

problems with boyfriends or
    girlfriends

appearance or image

fitting in

relationships in general

drama with friends

competition

In your school life

graduating

homework

grades

pressure to do well

pressure about college

bullying

sports

teachers or coaches

classes

pressure about your future

With your family

not feeling accepted

financial problems

responsibilities

rules

problems with parents

problems with siblings

problems with other family members

mental health difficulties

medical illness

Other

social media

spending too much time on
     technology

self-harm

figuring out who you are

fear of missing out

religious or spirituality issues

health and fitness

time management

sexuality

sexting

gender identity

self-confidence or self-esteem

online bullying

concerns about violence

Use these lines to add something that wasn't listed above or to explain in more detail
something you circled.

_____

_____

_____

_____

Sometimes you can't eliminate a stressor completely, but you can minimize its effect on you by spending less time thinking about it or by not being so involved with it.

Can you cut any of these stressors out of your life? If so, which ones?

_____

_____

Are there others you can change in some way, even if you can't cut them completely out of your life?

_____

_____

mindful takeaway   Although being aware of your stressors won't necessarily change their existence, this awareness can help empower you to take action and allow for change where possible.

something more

Stressors constantly change and fluctuate. The stressors you just circled most likely will not be the same ones you might circle next year, next month, next week—or even tomorrow. You will resolve some stressful situations, some new ones will arise, and some will persist for what feels like an eternity.

What stressed you out yesterday?

_____

_____

What stressed you out a week ago?

_____

_____

What stressed you out a month ago?

_____

_____

What stressed you out a year ago?

_____

_____

Which of these stressors no longer stress you out?

_____

_____

Did you resolve any of these? Tell how.

_____

_____

_____

Are you proud of how you handled any of these stressors? Tell about which ones, and why.

_____

_____

_____

mindful takeaway   Knowing the landscape of stressors that have been affecting your life provides you with information you can use for managing and coping with stressors.

At http://www.newharbinger.com/40187, you can download an additional activity, "Learning Who You Are," to help you learn more about who you are.

the physical effects of stress: paying attention to red flags 4

Your body gives you cues and signals letting you know when you are stressed. These cues and signals are red flags that can help you when you learn to identify them. When you feel threatened, your body automatically triggers what is called the *fight-or-flight stress response*. If you were a caveman hunting for food in prehistoric times and a saber-toothed tiger came into your path, your body would prepare to fight the tiger or to flee from it.

Fortunately, you won't run into a saber-toothed tiger these days. But your body reacts to almost every stressful moment in your life with that same response, as if you were encountering lots of tigers every day. For example, a bad grade on a test, a breakup with a girlfriend or boyfriend, accidentally posting a picture on social media, being followed on the street, or being startled by a noise when you're home alone can all cause your body to respond immediately with the fight-or-flight stress response.

Different people feel this response differently in their bodies. For example, you might find it harder to breathe, your hands might tingle, and your face might feel really hot and flushed. Your reaction(s) may also change at different points in time. One stressful situation might give you a stomachache, and another might make your shoulders tense. No matter what your physical signs, be aware that your body is letting you know it is stressed and wants to return to a more balanced and relaxed state—also known as *homeostasis*.

In the diagram that follows, the reactions listed on the left take place as your fight-or-flight stress response is triggered. After a while, these physical effects go away and your body goes back to a normal and more relaxed state, as shown on the right. On this diagram, mark where on your body you generally feel your stress.

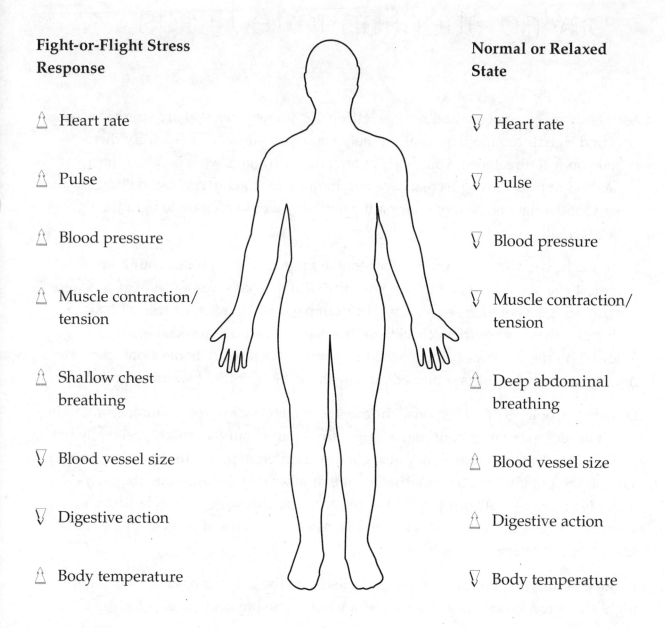

Fight-or-Flight Stress Response

⌃ Heart rate

⌃ Pulse

⌃ Blood pressure

⌃ Muscle contraction/ tension

⌃ Shallow chest breathing

⌄ Blood vessel size

⌄ Digestive action

⌃ Body temperature

Normal or Relaxed State

⌄ Heart rate

⌄ Pulse

⌄ Blood pressure

⌄ Muscle contraction/ tension

⌃ Deep abdominal breathing

⌃ Blood vessel size

⌃ Digestive action

⌄ Body temperature

The physical effects from the fight-or-flight stress response (such as your heart beating faster, your breathing becoming heavier, and your body temperature rising) are generally pretty short-lived. However, over time, stress has other, longer-lasting effects on the body.

Here is a list of physical symptoms that can be caused by stress. Some of these may last a few minutes or come and go, while others may last for days or even longer. Circle the symptoms you get when you are stressed. If you experience other physical problems that aren't listed, write them in.

stomachache

nausea

heartburn

muscle tightness

sweating

trembling

tingling or numbness

headache

change in appetite

unusually rapid speech

change in weight

change in sleep habits

change in skin: dryness, itchiness, rash

chest pains

dizziness, faintness, or weakness

throat feels like it is closing

shortness of breath or shallow breathing

heavy or faster breathing

racing or pounding heart

other: _____

other: _____

other: _____

mindful takeaway   At times, you might not even notice these physical red flags your body is raising to let you know that you are stressed. Or if you notice them, you might ignore them—not even on purpose. It is important to pay attention when your body is waving a red flag to indicate that you are stressed. It is a sign that you might need to change something in your life to get back to baseline.

something more

Mind-Body Connection

Although your head is connected to your body, there are many times when you can stay "up in your head" thinking and not notice the rest of your body. Your body is always there, giving you information about how you are doing, from normal to good to really bad. Paying attention to how your mind and body are connected can give you information about your stress level.

To notice your mind-body connection, you can use this practice below.

Whitney's Situation

Whitney's best friend, Natalie, decided she did not want to be friends with her anymore.

Whitney's Thoughts

What did I do wrong? I am not a good friend. Maybe I won't have friends anymore.

Maybe my other friends will stop liking me too. I am really unpopular. Everybody hates me!

Whitney's Feelings

I'm sad, upset, angry, and frustrated!

Whitney's Body

My shoulders are tense. It is kind of hard to breathe. I have tears in my eyes, and my body temperature must be rising because I can feel my face getting red.

Now try it yourself.

Describe a situation that you find particularly stressful at this moment.

_____

_____

When you think about this situation, what thoughts are coming up for you?

_____

_____

_____

What feelings are coming up for you about this situation?

_____

_____

How is your body affected?

_____

_____

_____

Is your body giving you any red flags that you are feeling different from when you are in a more normal, balanced state?

_____

_____

5 the emotional effects of stress

When you're feeling strong emotions—especially the "negative" ones—there's a good chance that stress is involved. Stress might make you feel depressed or worried. It can also affect you physically or your behavior, perhaps causing sleeplessness, nausea, or nail biting. It can even lead to such harmful behaviors as cutting, binge eating, or drug use.

Look at this list of feelings and think about which ones you have experienced when you were stressed. In the clouds on the following page, write down those feelings, or any others you may have had when you were stressed. If you need more room, write your other feelings around the clouds (or download another set of clouds from http://www.newharbinger.com/40187).

angry	scared
anxious	isolated or alone
depressed	overwhelmed
fearful	panicky
frustrated	restless
hopeless	sad
hostile	suspicious
jumpy	worried
nervous	worthless
numb	

Take a moment to reflect on what you see. You may have written down just a few feelings or so many that you are upset just looking at them. What thoughts and feelings are coming up for you right now?

_____

_____

_____

_____

Now focus on the positive, and notice all the feelings from the list that you haven't experienced as part of stress.

mindful takeaway   Your mind and body provide red flags, cues, and signals when you are angry, sad, or depressed, but you may not pay attention or notice them. Tuning into these signals will give you information that can help you start doing things differently to change and manage your stress.

something more

Sometimes you can physically feel your emotional pain. For example, instead of crying you might have a stomachache or a headache. Emotional pain eventually finds a way out even if you are trying to squash it. It is similar to a pot of water that is being heated by a flame: it will eventually boil, and if it is not attended to, the water will boil over.

In the outline below (also available at http://www.newharbinger.com/40187), mark or color the parts of your body where you can feel your emotional pain. Try using different colors to help you express your moods and feelings.

Looking at what you just drew, how do you feel now?

_____

_____

What in your life would you like to change or be different?

_____

_____

What, if anything, have you learned about yourself?

_____

_____

What can you take away from this drawing activity?

_____

_____

6   when stress can be helpful

Stress can provide cues and red flags that can actually help you perform and do better in different activities: homework, taking tests, and even sports or music competitions.

When Stress Helps

> *Andrew plays soccer on his school's team. He tends to get really nervous before a game, and his stomach often feels a little queasy. At the same time, his adrenaline increases and that helps him perform better.*

Andrew found that these stress cues helped him perform better. In other cases when you get too stressed, you may go beyond a helpful point and the balance tips; then stress gets too great. Stress begins to decrease your ability to do well and starts to harm you.

When Stress Harms

> *Samantha tends to put school assignments off until the last minute. Sometimes waiting until close to the deadline works in her favor; she gets her homework done, and the pressure helps her do it well. At other times, she waits too long, and the stress is so great that she can't finish her homework and gives up altogether.*

These additional examples will help you see how stress can help or harm.

You get named the captain of the football team.

Helpful Stress: You are proud of this position, and the stress motivates you to work harder and do better on the team because of it.

Harmful Stress: You get so nervous that you start to play worse.

You get a really difficult homework assignment.

Helpful Stress: You feel challenged by this assignment and spend extra effort on it because you want to do well and are interested in the topic.

Harmful Stress: You are so overwhelmed that you give up and don't even do the assignment.

Tell about a time when stress helped you perform better or increased your motivation.

_____

_____

_____

_____

Can you think of a time when you passed that helpful point and the stress actually began to harm you? Describe what happened.

_____

_____

_____

_____

something more

There may be times when you could use stress to your advantage but aren't currently. Can you think of times when stress could help you in each of these areas?

At school: _____

_____

After school: _____

_____

At home: _____

_____

With your friends: _____

_____

In your extracurricular life (activities, hobbies, and interests): _____

_____

_____

Other: _____

_____

stress the problem, mindfulness a solution

7

You have now learned how stressed you are, what you are stressed by, and how your body experiences stress: physically, mentally, and/or emotionally. This information is the first step in managing your stress. You now have the ability to recognize what is going on and can decide how you want to respond to it. You aren't powerless!

The stressors you are experiencing and the stress they are causing are the problems, and one possible solution for changing and taking control of that stress is through learning about and using mindfulness.

Mindfulness is noticing your thoughts, feelings, and physical sensations in the present moment.

Have you ever been in a car and arrived at your destination without noticing how you got there? Your answer to this question is probably yes. Mindfulness allows you to notice your life as it is actually taking place; in this case, it means noticing how you got to your destination or realizing that you didn't notice how you got there.

Why practice mindfulness?

- It will help you be in the here and now.

- You will be more aware of how you are doing physically, mentally, and emotionally.

- You will be able to choose how you want to respond to life's situations.

- Insight into how you are doing can help you make more thoughtful decisions.

When you are mindful, you are more:

- thoughtful

- focused

- aware, present

- responsive

When you aren't mindful, you are more:

- mindless

- distracted, inattentive

- on automatic pilot

- reactive, impulsive

Why you might find it hard to be mindful:

- You don't want to feel something.

- You don't want to notice what is going on right now.

- You want to escape.

- You don't want to deal with stuff right now.

Although it can be especially difficult to pay attention to painful emotions or situations you would rather not have in your life, information and knowledge about a situation can be powerful. The more you know about a situation, the more control you have over the decisions you make.

What are some things taking place in your life right now that you might not want to be present for, aware of, or mindful of?

_____

_____

_____

_____

What are some events in your life that are causing you pain, stress, or suffering?

_____

_____

_____

How do you usually manage painful emotions or situations?

_____

_____

_____

something more

Types of Mindfulness Practice

There are two types of mindfulness practice: formal and informal. In *formal practice*, you actually set aside a specific amount of time and dedicate it to being mindful. *Informal practice* doesn't require any extra time. You can bring informal practice to your day-to-day activities.

The upcoming formal and informal mindfulness practices are some of the tools you can implement to change and reduce your pain, stress, and suffering.

mindful takeaway   Information and knowledge about a situation can be powerful. The more you know about a person, place, or thing, the more power and control you have over the decisions you make.

Visit http://www.newharbinger.com/40187 for an activity that can help you boost your creativity and step outside the house with the activity "Step Outside the Box."

living in the now 8

Have you ever found yourself staring at a screen, forgetting what you were doing because you were deep in thought about something else? This is an example of not being aware, present, or in the moment.

The essence of mindfulness is to bring awareness to everything you do in life. It is in the here and now that you live. It is normal and natural to zone out, but if you are frequently on automatic pilot during the day, think of all you might be missing!

To help you start living in the now, take from one to three minutes and write down all the thoughts that come to your mind. Your grammar doesn't matter. Just write one thought on each line as it comes up.

Now, next to each thought, write the letter *P* if the thought is a thought from the past, write the letter *N* if it is a thought in the now, and write the letter *F* if the thought is about something in the future. If you need more room, get a separate piece of paper.

_____

_____

_____

_____

mindful takeaway   When you spend so much time thinking about what has already happened (things you can't change) or what is going to happen, you are missing out on your life right now! Thoughts about your past can often include replaying what has already happened or worrying or judging how you did or performed. Thoughts about your future can often include worries about how something will turn out, and worrying will not change how something actually turns out.

something more

Take a look at your thoughts on the previous page and count the Ps, Ns, and Fs.

Notice how many thoughts are actually in the now, the Ns.

What are you missing when you are focused on your thoughts about the past or about the future?

_____

_____

_____

mindful takeaway   Thinking about what has happened or worrying about what is going to happen isn't often helpful or productive, and it is often judgmental and destructive to you. When you catch yourself ruminating about the past or worrying about the future, pay attention to something in the now (for example, your body or the room you are in) to help ground you in the here and now.

mindfulness and the five senses

When you are stressed, it might seem difficult to be mindful, but it can be pretty simple. When you notice any of your senses, you are in the present; you are mindful of something right now in this very moment.

There are five senses you can pay attention to:

- sight
- smell
- touch
- taste
- hearing

Right now, write down what you:

1. See

What do you see around you, behind you, on you, right in front of you?

_____

2. Smell

What do you smell? You might want to close your eyes.

_____

3. Touch

What do your clothes feel like? What are you in contact with: a chair or some other object? What position are you in: sitting, lying down, or some other position? What do you feel with your hands? With other parts of your body?

_____

4. Taste

What do you taste? Can you taste the air? Can you taste something you recently ate or drank?

_____

5. Hear

What do you hear? It might help to close your eyes.

_____

By focusing on your five senses, what did you notice that you hadn't noticed before?

_____

_____

Perhaps you were unable to notice anything with one or more of your senses. That is perfectly normal. Just notice what the absence of sight, smell, touch, taste, and sound is like.

something more

Here are some ways to do something beneficial or positive for yourself while using your five senses.

What you see

- Make one area of your bedroom neat, without anything cluttering it.

- Buy or pick a beautiful flower.

- Sit outside and notice nature around you (the sky, the sun, the grass, the trees, or the stars at night).

- Look at cool pictures online or at photographs of you or your friends.

- Notice any of your own drawings that you like.

- Go to a museum and observe a piece of artwork that appeals to you.

- Look at familiar objects (a television, a computer, a cell phone) and find details you hadn't noticed before.

What you smell

- Smell your favorite perfume or cologne.

- Notice the scent of your soap or lotion.

- Light an aromatic candle and notice the fragrance.

- Sniff flowers.

- Smell the outdoors (the grass of the football field, the chlorine of a swimming pool).

- Take a walk outside or even in the woods and notice the fresh smells.

- Pay attention to the smells of food, from freshly baked cookies to garlic and onions.

What you touch

- Notice what it feels like to hug someone or give someone a high five.

- Put clean sheets on your bed and be aware of how they feel when you first get in.

- Pay attention to what it feels like to be warm or cold.

- Notice the feel of your favorite pair of jeans.

- Feel the warmth of a shower.

- Pet your pet.

- Sit in a really comfortable chair.

- Walk on grass with your bare feet.

What you taste

- Taste all the food you eat; really taste it.

- Enjoy every bite of your favorite food.

- Savor a sweet bite of chocolate.

- Chew a piece of gum or suck on your favorite mint.

What you hear

- Listen to a great song that is soothing or invigorating.

- Sing a favorite song by yourself or with some friends.

- Pay attention to the sounds of nature (rain, birds chirping, leaves rustling, waves crashing).

- Learn to play an instrument, or if you already play, really listen to yourself.

- Become aware of sounds you usually hear automatically (the phone ringing, the signal of a text, the bell at school, the engine of a car).

bringing mindfulness to routine tasks and interests 10

People often do things without being fully aware of what they are doing, as if they were on automatic pilot. Living this way, they cheat themselves out of many moments in their lives. Trying to bring conscious awareness to your body and mind while remaining aware of the task you are engaging in will allow you to experience life more fully. The idea is to bring moment-to-moment awareness to everything you do in life and to zero in on what you are doing as you are actually doing it.

Being Mindful of Routine Activities

There are many tasks you do frequently, for example, brushing your teeth, taking a shower, and getting dressed. Although these tasks are routine, you can still be mindful when you do them. Who knows? You might notice something you hadn't before.

Below is a list of some routine activities that you can bring mindful awareness to; you can use the blank lines to add others. When you pay attention to any of your five senses while engaging in any of these activities, you are being mindful.

- waking up
- brushing your teeth
- showering
- shaving
- brushing your hair
- getting dressed
- tying your shoes
- washing your hands
- eating
- messaging, posting
- walking to class
- shopping
- dancing
- riding in a car
- working out
- taking your dog for a walk

- brushing a pet
- folding laundry
- taking out the garbage
- washing dishes
- cleaning your room
- being with friends or family
- writing
- journaling
- drawing
- playing a musical instrument
- playing a sport
- getting into bed
- going to sleep
- other: _____
- other: _____
- other: _____

The next time you do one of these activities, do your best to pay attention with your five senses while you're doing it. Answer the questions below.

What routine activity did you choose?

_____

What did you see?

_____

What did you smell?

_____

What did you touch?

_____

What did you taste?

_____

What did you hear?

_____

mindful takeaway   Every time you do this activity during the next week, bring mindful awareness to it using your five senses. Once you feel comfortable doing this activity mindfully, try another.

Being Mindful of Your Interests

Mindfulness is not just for routine activities. It can also apply to your hobbies, extracurricular activities, and interests.

Bianca enjoys playing the guitar as a way to chill out. She wants to bring mindfulness to this interest. She can do this through paying attention to her five senses.

Sight

She sees the guitar, the strings, the wood, the sound hole, the pick, the pick guard, and the tuning knobs. She also sees where the guitar is placed on her lap. She notices the colors around her—on the guitar, her clothes, the cushion, and the walls.

Smell

As she puts the guitar to her nose and sniffs, she recognizes the smell of what she knows to be wood. She also smells the candle that she has lit on the desk and the air of the room.

Touch

She feels the strings and the difference between all of them. She feels a few rough edges where the guitar has been worn. She notices how her clothes feel loose.

Taste

She tastes the coffee she drank about twenty minutes ago. Its once-strong taste has faded.

Hearing

As she plucks the strings, she hears the sounds her guitar is making. In the background, she hears the hum of the air conditioner.

Going through this process allowed Bianca to notice many details she had been missing. For her, playing guitar holds renewed interest.

Write down a few of your interests:

_____

_____

_____

Pick one of these interests and pay attention to your five senses while you do it.

What interest did you choose?

_____

What did you see?

_____

_____

_____

What did you smell?

_____

_____

_____

What did you touch?

_____

_____

_____

What did you taste?

_____

_____

_____

What did you hear?

_____

_____

_____

something more

Mindful Music Practice

First: Pick one of your favorite songs. Go listen to that song, and don't continue reading here until it is over.

✱ ✱ ✱

Second: This time, listen to the same song mindfully and do your best to notice all five of your senses. List below what you noticed with each of your senses.

Try being mindful of music.

What did you see?

_____

_____

_____

What did you smell?

_____

_____

_____

What did you touch?

_____

_____

_____

What did you taste?

_____

_____

_____

What did you hear?

_____

_____

_____

What did you notice when you listened to the song mindfully? What was different?
What was the same?

_____

_____

_____

dropping-in mindfulness practice 11

Zoe plays lacrosse, goes to school, babysits for some extra cash, and is the treasurer of her junior class. She is so busy that she doesn't know when she can take time to be mindful. Luckily, she doesn't have to make extra time to be mindful.

Being mindful is as simple as 1–2–3. Notice your:

1. Body

2. Breath

3. Mind

You can do the dropping-in mindfulness practice anytime you want; it doesn't require you to set aside a specific amount of time to be mindful. This practice is about dropping in to this moment, and noticing your body, breath, and mind as each is right now. Each time you do this activity, what you notice will be different depending on your circumstances. Depending on how long you have, you can do this practice as quickly as you can say 1–2–3, or you can slow it down, spending more time on each of the three sections.

If you have time, ask yourself the questions after each section and write about your experience. If you don't have the time, skip the questions, and move on to the next section.

Dropping-In Mindfulness Practice

1. Body

Take a minute right now to scan your body, from the tips of your toes moving up to the top of your head. Notice what you feel in your body.

Where are you right now (location)?

What position is your body in (standing, sitting, lying down)?

What is the temperature, and how does that affect your body?

What time of day is it: morning, afternoon, or evening?

Are you inside or outdoors?

Does anything ache or hurt?

Do you notice a pain you didn't know was there before?

Does your body feel the way it normally does?

What did you notice in your body?

_____

_____

_____

_____

2. **Breath**

Take a minute right now and notice your breath. Try not to change your breathing. Sometimes it can be hard to notice your breathing without changing it, but you want to try to be an observer of your breath as it is happening, so just notice it as it is. If you have changed your breathing, and it feels restricted, sharp, or shallow, this is fine too. During repeated practice of noticing your breath, you will find you can notice your breath without changing the pattern that is normal for you. It can help to notice your stomach rise on the in-breath and gently fall on the out-breath.

You can pay attention to where you inhale and exhale: is it your nose or mouth?

Is your breath cool or warm?

Does your breath feel restricted, sharp, or shallow?

Is it hard to notice your breath without changing it?

Were you able to get to a point where you noticed your breath and didn't change it?

Did you observe your stomach moving up and down as you were breathing?

Did you notice your heart beating when you noticed your breath?

Did you notice your chest move?

What did you notice about your breath?

_____

_____

_____

_____

_____

3. Mind

Notice what is going on in your mind. Take up to a minute to notice what you are feeling and thinking right now. Answer the following questions on the lines below.

What feelings did you notice?

What are you feeling right now?

Do you have a hard time identifying or knowing how you are feeling right now?

Are you feeling what people often refer to as a good emotion (for example, happiness, joy, contentment, or peacefulness)?

Are you feeling what people often refer to as a bad emotion (for example, sadness or anger)?

_____

_____

_____

_____

What thoughts did you notice?

What are you thinking about right now?

Are your thoughts about the past, now, and/or future?

Are your thoughts worrisome or judgmental?

_____

_____

_____

_____

What are some of your takeaways from doing the dropping-in mindfulness practice?

_____

_____

_____

_____

_____

_____

mindful takeaway   Your body gives you information. If you start checking in with it frequently, you will learn what your body feels like when it is "normal" and when something is out of balance or "off." In this way, you can use your detective skills to let you know when you aren't feeling right and adjust accordingly.

something more

Dropping-In Mindfulness Practice for Sleep

Do you ever have a hard time falling asleep because your to-do list is running through your mind or you can't stop thinking about what took place during your day? Do you have a hard time relaxing or chilling out enough to sleep? If so, the dropping-in practice can help.

Before you go to sleep, drop in to your

1. body,

2. breath, and

3. mind

Body

Get into a comfortable sleeping position. Make sure your clothes, blankets, and pillows are the way you like them. Check everything out and adjust everything to get to a "Yes, I'm comfortable" position.

Scan your body from the tips of your toes to the top of your head, and notice how you feel. Do you feel tense or tight? Do you have pain? Adjust yourself accordingly.

Breath

Notice your breath just as it is in this moment. Count your breaths as you notice them. You can say to yourself, *Breathing in one, breathing out one, breathing in two, breathing out two*. Continue to count for three to five breaths.

When you checked in with your body, did you notice any areas of pain or discomfort? Imagine that your next in-breath brings soothing air to areas that felt discomfort. On the out-breath, imagine the air carrying away that discomfort.

Mind

Turn your cell phone and other technology off, or put them on silent. If you have the capability to change your screen setting to dim at night, do that. Before you go to sleep, you will have thoughts and feelings. Just notice them. Sometimes when you fight not to have them or wish for them to go away, it is almost impossible to get that result.

mindful takeaway   Just notice what you are thinking and feeling. You can say to yourself, *Oh, interesting. This is what I'm thinking and feeling right now.* Then you can return to counting your breaths if it helps.

12 mindful eating practice

Mindful eating, a formal mindfulness practice, involves noticing how and what you eat, from one bite to an entire meal. People often don't notice what they are eating or whether they are still hungry. While they are eating, they may be listening to music, doing homework, or busy with their phone, tablet, or computer. Taking time to eat your food mindfully, you can begin to learn what foods actually taste like and which foods you like and dislike. What if you just ate and did nothing else for a change?

Mindful Eating Practice

1. To eat mindfully, get three pieces of some snack food (for example, nuts or raisins). Look at this food as something new you have never seen, even if you have eaten it a thousand times. Before you begin to eat, notice what is around you in the room and what thoughts and feelings you have. Notice your breathing as you inhale and exhale a few times.

2. Set two pieces of the food aside, and take the third in your hand. Look at what you are about to eat. Think about how it got to you, from a field or store all the way to your hand. How do you feel knowing that you are going to eat? What do you notice in your mind?

3. Use your five senses. Notice what the piece looks like. Roll it around in your hand. What does it feel like? Hold it to your nose. What does it smell like? Place it near your ear. Can you hear anything? If you move it between your fingers, does it make a sound?

4. Feel the piece with your lips, and notice the taste it has left on them. Put it into your mouth without chewing it. What do you notice starting to take place in your mouth? Close your eyes, and let the piece roll around on your tongue. Put it between your teeth and feel it there without biting into it yet. Is your mouth watering? Pay attention to the change in its texture after it has been in your mouth for a bit.

5. Bite into the piece, noticing any tastes you experience. Slowly chew it for as long as you can. Right before you swallow, notice what it feels like to want to swallow this food. When you are ready, go ahead and swallow.

Notes: When you notice yourself getting distracted by your thoughts or feelings, take a moment to notice the distraction and refocus on the food. Repeat this process with the remaining two pieces of food.

You can follow these steps with any food of your choosing, from one bite to an entire meal.

What food was it that you ate mindfully?

_____

_____

What changes did you notice in the food as you ate (texture, taste, size, and shape)?

_____

_____

If you have had this food before, what was similar or different when you ate it mindfully?

_____

_____

Describe how you typically eat—quickly, slowly, and so on.

_____

_____

What other foods could you try to eat mindfully?

_____

_____

What are you going to eat mindfully this week?

_____

_____

mindful takeaway   This week, try eating one bite of every meal mindfully. Start to notice what foods actually taste like when you eat them mindfully. You might notice that a food you thought you liked tastes unpleasant and that you actually don't like that food.

something more

Stress Eating

Stress eating is when people turn to food as a comfort to relieve stress. This means that they eat more food than they need or want to get a sense of relief from or control over outside stressors.

Consider these two questions:

- Do you eat more when you are stressed?

- Do you eat to change your mood?

If you answered yes to either of these questions, you are most likely stress eating.

You can use mindful eating to develop an awareness of your eating habits. Each time you are going to eat over the next week, ask yourself:

- What is it that I am about to eat?

- Am I eating because I am hungry?

- Am I eating because I am stressed and want food to help me feel better?

After you have thought about these questions, if you are eating because you are hungry and not because you are stressed, eat. If you are eating because you are stressed and doing so to feel better, consider talking with a mental health professional or an adult you trust.

13 the body scan mindfulness practice

The body scan is a formal mindfulness practice. It takes you on a tour through your body from the tips of your toes to the top of your head. The point of this practice is to be aware of your mind and body as one. Let go of expectations of a right or wrong way to practice; whatever you experience is fine.

The best place to do a body scan is somewhere with the fewest distractions. This includes distractions from other people, technology, and noise. Wherever it is, make sure you feel safe and comfortable.

It's likely that you'll need to look at these instructions the first few times you do this mindfulness practice. As you get used to doing it, you may be able to do the body scan without having to read these instructions. When you can do that, you might want to close your eyes.

During all practices, always feel free to readjust yourself to be more comfortable. If you ever feel a practice is harming you, go ahead and stop the practice altogether!

The Body Scan Mindfulness Practice

Time allotted: 8–15 minutes

Start with a shorter time, and as you get used to doing it, feel free to increase your time. You can use an alarm to help keep track of time.

1. **Get into position; get comfortable.**

   Lie down on your back or sit in a comfortable position. A pillow or blanket might help you get more comfortable. Take a minute to notice the points of contact your body has with the surface you are on, whether it is a bed, the floor, a chair, or some other location. Feel your whole body.

2. **Notice your breath in your body.**

   Begin to notice your breath, feeling it as it moves through your body. You might feel the air as it moves through your nose or mouth. Notice the feeling of your belly rising on the in-breath and gently falling on the out-breath. Don't try to change your breathing, and if it changes, just notice the difference.

   If you have a pain or discomfort, imagine the air from your in-breath focusing in on that part of the body. On the out-breath, imagine the discomfort leaving with the air.

3. **Notice your feet and legs.**

   Now focus on the tips of your toes on your right foot. Try to feel each toe and the spaces between your toes without moving them. Picture your breath at the tips of your toes. Slowly move your awareness to the bottom of your right foot, to the ball of your foot, and then to your heel and what it is in contact with right now. If you can't feel much of anything, that's fine; just notice what it feels like to feel nothing. After a few moments, move to the top of your right foot and ankle.

   Continue on through your lower right leg, your calf muscle, your knee, and your upper thigh. Notice all the muscles in your leg. Try to feel any contact your right leg has with the surface you are on. Once you have reached your right hip, move across to your left hip and down to the toes of your left foot, and repeat with your left side what you just did with your right side. Once you have reached your hip on your left leg, focus your awareness on both your legs. Think of the support your feet and legs provide every day. Breathe in to your feet and legs on the next in-breath, and release anything you choose on the next out-breath.

4. **Notice your stomach and chest.**

Move to your abdomen and lower stomach, again noticing the rise and fall of your belly as you breathe. As you move up to your chest, lungs, and ribs, notice them expand and release as you breathe. Try to feel your heartbeat. Move your attention to the top of your chest and to your collarbone.

5. **Notice your hands and arms.**

From your collarbone, move to your right shoulder and bring your attention down to the tips of your fingers on your right hand. Try to feel each finger and the spaces between them, without moving them. Pay attention to the air around your fingers and to any contact your right hand has with anything else. Notice any sensations in your hand, and focus your awareness on them. Move up through your palm and the back of your hand to your wrist, forearm, elbow, upper right arm, and shoulder. Once you have reached your right shoulder, move across to the left shoulder and down to the tips of your fingers on your left hand, and repeat with your left side what you just did with your right side.

6. **Notice your back.**

Now bring your attention to your shoulders, and then to your back and down to the bottom of your lower back. Slowly moving up your back, from the tailbone all the way to your shoulders and neck, notice every vertebra and muscle you encounter as you move up to your shoulders. Imagine that someone was gently pulling at the top of your head and you had a bit of space between each of your vertebrae, and notice each and every vertebra as you move to the top of your back. Breathe in to any tension or tightness you have in your back or shoulders, bringing in fresh air on your next in-breath and releasing any tension or tightness you have on your next out-breath.

7. **Notice your neck and head.**

Slowly move up to the back of your neck and head. Try to notice the hair on your head. Move toward the front of your face. If you are holding a facial expression, let it go. If you are clenching your jaw, release it. Now notice your forehead, temples, eyebrows, eyelashes, and eyes. Notice what you see through your closed eyelids. Notice your ears, cheeks, nose, nostrils, mouth, lips, teeth, tongue, jaw, chin, and finally your throat.

8. **Notice your entire body.**

   Now focus your awareness on your entire body from the tips of your toes to the top of your head. Imagine a tiny hole the size of a quarter on the top of your head, like a dolphin's blowhole. Imagine breathing in air through this hole, then gently moving the air all the way through your body and out through the tips of your toes.

9. **Concluding Your Practice**

   Notice how you feel at this very moment. To bring yourself back from this mindfulness practice, gently wiggle your toes and/or begin to move your fingers. If your eyes are closed, slowly open them when you are ready and come back to the room you are in.

You completed your body scan mindfulness practice—congratulations! Remember, you can take a piece of how you feel right now with you to the rest of your day if you so choose.

Mindfulness Practice Debriefing

What did it feel like to notice the different parts of your body?

_____

_____

Sometimes people have a hard time focusing on their bodies. How did it feel to focus on your body?

_____

_____

What physical sensations did you notice (the desire to move or adjust your body, any physical discomfort)?

_____

_____

What thoughts came up for you?

_____

_____

_____

When you got distracted or your mind wandered, were you able to gently bring your attention back to your breath and body? What was that like?

_____

_____

_____

What feelings came up for you?

_____

_____

_____

If you felt any emotional discomfort, what was that like?

_____

_____

_____

Part of this experience is to just be with all that comes up for you. What do you think about this mindfulness practice?

_____

_____

_____

mindful takeaway   Each time you do the body scan practice, your experience will be different from any previous experience. There is no right or wrong way to feel during or after a mindfulness practice. You might label a practice as good or bad, but remember that whatever you experience is normal. Try this practice a handful of times, and notice how different the experience is each time.

something more

To have an audio version of this practice, you can record the guided body scan instructions as you read them aloud. Or you can record them while a partner reads the instructions as you do the practice. Pick a partner you trust and feel comfortable with.

mindful takeaway   The body scan practice is often very helpful to use before you go to sleep at night. It can calm down the to-do list or the worries inside your head.

bringing mindfulness to walking and movement 14

Have you ever walked someplace and not realized how you got there? This is an example of being on automatic pilot. When you walk to class, to your locker, or to lunch, you obviously get from point A to point B. You might even have a brief interaction with a friend along the way without paying much attention to it. Walking mindfully allows you to use movement to bring yourself into the present moment.

Mindful Walking Practice

1. Choose a path about ten feet long; it can be anywhere you will be safe—inside or outside of your home or school, for example. The overall path doesn't have to be long because you are not trying to get anywhere. It is about being mindful of the movement, not to how far you have gone. If you want to walk barefoot, take off your shoes.

2. For five to ten minutes, slowly walk back and forth on this path. Move your arms in whatever ways are comfortable to you. Start to experience what it is like to just walk and notice the sensations of actually walking. Notice what it feels like to lift your foot, shift, move, and place your foot; then start again with the other foot. You might want to attend to what causes your leg to lift or what sensations you have in your body. At the end of your path, turn around, paying as much attention to the process of turning as you did to walking.

3. If your mind wanders while you are walking, that's normal; it's what minds do. When a thought, a feeling, or something else distracts you in your surroundings, give yourself permission to stop walking. Take a moment to pay attention to whatever thought, feeling, or other thing distracted you, and then continue walking. What is important is the awareness that you got distracted and started walking again. Each time you engage in a walking mindfulness practice, try not to evaluate how you did. There is no good or bad way to do this practice.

What was it like to walk like this?

_____

_____

_____

Some people are so used to walking at a certain pace that slowing down makes them feel off balance. If you felt off balance walking slowly, describe that experience.

_____

_____

_____

What was it like walking with no end point or destination to get to?

_____

_____

_____

What thoughts did you notice?

_____

_____

_____

What distracted you?

_____

_____

_____

What feelings came up for you during the walking practice?

_____

_____

_____

List a few places where you would like to try walking mindfully.

_____

_____

_____

mindful takeaway   Your feet, like your breath, are always with you. If you just notice them, your feet can be your anchor point to ground you in this moment.

something more

You can be mindful of all the places you walk and to all physical activities you engage in. It is about bringing mindful attention and presence to all movement. You don't have to be slow to be mindful! You can notice the activity you are doing, your breath, your body, and where your mind wanders.

During the week, practice bringing mindful awareness to some physical activity you do, and write about what your experience is. Use your senses (sight, sound, taste, touch, and smell) to guide you in these activities.

_____

_____

_____

_____

_____

_____

doing homework or taking a test mindfully 15

You can bring mindful presence to anything you do, including homework and tests.

Mindful Homework or Test Taking Practice

Follow these steps to help you center yourself *before* you begin your homework or start to take a test. If you find yourself getting tense or stressed while in the middle of your work, you can repeat this process at any time.

1. Get into a comfortable sitting position.

2. Place your hands in your lap or on your desk.

3. Open your ears to the sounds you notice, and allow yourself to be in the room right here, right now.

4. Pay attention to your breath without changing it in any way if you can. If you can't, just notice that too.

5. Notice how your stomach gently rises on the in-breath and falls on the out-breath.

6. Notice how your body feels from the tips of your toes to the top of your head—quickly scanning your body.

7. If you feel nervous or anxious (or have any other feelings that aren't productive or helpful), take one deep intentional breath. As you slowly release this breath, imagine that you are gently breathing out these feelings.

8. Take your next breath, and picture ease and peace coming in.

9. Imagine yourself doing your homework assignment or taking your test with ease.

10. Imagine yourself gently putting down your pen or pencil or lifting your hands from the keyboard, and when you are done, acknowledge putting forth the effort to do your best and complete the task.

You are now ready to begin (or return to) your homework assignment or test. If you feel uncomfortable or stuck while you're working, remember that you can take another breath at any time or even repeat the whole process.

mindful takeaway   Negative thoughts about how you are going to do on your homework or test can often impact how you actually do. When you notice yourself having negative thoughts, remember to notice your breath, focus on your body, and start on your task again. Referring back to the dropping-in mindfulness practice can also help.

something more

Once you have had the opportunity to try this exercise, explain how taking a test or doing your homework mindfully was different.

_____

_____

_____

_____

Consider the space in which you do your homework. A well organized, confortable space can really help. Are there any changes you can make to the areas where you work? Write your ideas here.

_____

_____

_____

_____

accepting your emotions: 16
"the guest house"

When people are filled with difficult emotions, they often cling to them or push them away. Emotions can be recognized, labeled, and learned from, even when they are unpleasant and uncomfortable.

Keep in mind that this poem was originally written in the 1200s. Yes, that's right—the 1200s. Please read it aloud or silently two times.

"The Guest House"

This being human is a guest house.
Every morning a new arrival.

A joy, a depression, a meanness,
some momentary awareness comes
as an unexpected visitor.

Welcome and entertain them all!
Even if they're a crowd of sorrows,
who violently sweep your house
empty of its furniture,
still, treat each guest honorably.
He may be clearing you out
for some new delight.

The dark thought, the shame, the malice,
meet them at the door laughing, and invite them in.

Be grateful for whoever comes,
because each has been sent
as a guide from beyond.

—Rumi

What do you think this poem means? There are no right or wrong answers; just share what it means to you.

_____

_____

_____

What feelings are in your guest house right now?

_____

_____

_____

Write about how you might process unwanted feelings by taking them in as information and nothing more.

_____

_____

_____

How do you currently deal with negative emotions?

_____

_____

_____

Rumi's poem suggests that negative emotions "may be clearing you out for some new delight." What does this mean to you?

_____

_____

_____

If you apply this quotation to yourself, can you think of what your new delight could be?

_____

_____

_____

Having negative or unpleasant moments can help you know what other moments are positive or pleasant. What does this mean to you?

_____

_____

_____

What does being "grateful for whoever comes, because each has been sent as a guide from beyond" mean to you?

_____

_____

_____

something more

In the space below, draw a picture of a house that represents your emotional state right now.

Explain on the lines below, what is going on in your guest house.

_____

_____

_____

What feelings are present for you?

_____

_____

_____

What thoughts come up for you?

_____

_____

_____

If you want to, you can write these feelings or thoughts in the house you drew.

17 don't believe everything you think

What if a thought were just a thought and nothing more? You may be giving more power to your thoughts than you need to. What if when you became aware of a thought, you didn't add to it but just noticed it?

In the middle of doing her homework, Diane thinks that no one likes her.

A thought is just a thought, not truth, fact, or reality.

Diane notices herself having the thought that no one likes her and continues to do her homework.

Adding more to the thought than you need to can lead to feelings that bring you down.

Diane stops doing her homework. She begins to think about all the times in the past that she has lost a friend. She also thinks about her current group of friends and assumes that she knows what each person thinks of her. These thoughts support her original idea that no one likes her. She starts to feel sad and tired.

When Diane kept thinking about friends she had lost, she began to feel depressed, worthless, sad, and tired.

Write for one minute about the thoughts you are having right now.

_____

_____

_____

_____

Can you see places where you might blow some of these thoughts out of proportion? If so, explain.

_____

_____

_____

What are some feelings that went along with the thoughts you just wrote about above?

_____

_____

_____

Try expanding your feelings vocabulary. Circle any of the feelings below that often describe how you feel.

Words of anxiety

> *I feel worried, anxious, afraid, threatened, cautious, hesitant, distrustful, embarrassed, freaked out, and uneasy.*

Words of happiness

> *I feel excited, joyful, lucky, satisfied, pleased, hopeful, relieved, delighted, and cheerful.*

Words of sadness

> *I feel bummed out, depressed, unhappy, disappointed, hurt, hopeless, lonely, miserable, negative, lost, crushed, and helpless.*

Words of anger

> *I feel mad, bitter, annoyed, irritable, impatient, aggressive, frustrated, vengeful, and enraged.*

Choosing from the lists above, what feelings have you had today?

_____

_____

_____

What thoughts come up when you think of each of the feelings you had today?

_____

_____

_____

What feelings words would you say you most often use to describe yourself?

_____

_____

_____

_____

mindful takeaway   What you think affects how you feel, and how you feel affects what you think. Feelings and thoughts are connected even if they seem separate.

something more

Psychologist Rick Hanson writes, "We are Velcro to the negative and Teflon to the positive." It is often very easy to find the negative qualities and beliefs about yourself and very hard to think about your strengths and positive qualities. Give it a try and see this quotation in action. In the space below, write down all your negative qualities and all your positive qualities.

Negative Qualities	Positive Qualities

Which list is longer?

_____

What do you notice when you read these lists?

_____

_____

_____

What do you feel in your body?

_____

_____

What thoughts come up for you?

_____

_____

_____

_____

What feelings come up for you?

_____

_____

_____

Learn more about your perceived strengths and weaknesses with the activity, "Perceptions or Fact? Your Strengths and Weakness," at http://www.newharbinger. com/40187.

mindful takeaway   A judgment is a type of thought, and just because you have the thought doesn't mean it is true or real.

don't jump on the train of thoughts: the railroad activity 18

People spend a lot of time ruminating and worrying. When they do this, it can make it difficult to pay attention to or enjoy what they're currently doing, or even just relax.

When Bailey went to bed at night, she had a very hard time falling asleep. Her to-do list would pop up, and it would take her a long time to get it to go away. When she got up in the morning, she was often really tired.

Learning to observe your thoughts as they arise—without clinging or adding to them or trying to ignore or push them away—can reduce your stress.

Railroad Activity Practice

Seated in a comfortable position, imagine yourself sitting on top of a hill.

Once you have this image in your mind, look down at the bottom of the hill and see a train track. Picture a train starting to pass.

As you see each car go by, think of each as one of your thoughts.

Without jumping onto the train, notice the cars—your thoughts—as they pass.

If you find that one thought keeps popping back up, just notice it.

You can say, *Oh, interesting. This is what I am thinking right now* and return to noticing your train as it is passing by.

Bailey tried this exercise. She found that when she just noticed her thoughts without telling herself, I need to stop thinking about this or that, *it helped her get off the train of thoughts.*

Bailey began to notice her thoughts as train cars, separate from herself. When she was able to let the thoughts pass by, this helped reduce her stress, worries, and anxiety.

You can also use this practice during any of your other mindfulness practices when you find yourself distracted by your thoughts, specifically when you are ruminating, worrying, and the like.

mindful takeaway   Sometimes it helps to write a list of all your to-dos, and then put the list away until you can actually work on it. If it is at night, put the list away until tomorrow. Each idea or item to do will still be there, and you don't have to worry about forgetting it as it is now written down.

something more

Draw the train that was in your mind. On the picture of the train, write the thoughts that often come up for you and make it hard for you to relax.

When you notice these thoughts, just let them pass as a train passes by.

19 stress waves: riding the waves of life

Imagine being on a rowboat in the ocean. The waves in the ocean represent everything causing you stress right now: your *stress waves*. The waves might be calm and still or crashing, fierce, and rough. A large number of waves equals many events and stressors in your life.

Jon wants very much to please his parents by getting into college. He believes he has to get good grades, play sports, and be in a number of clubs to get accepted. He feels like he has no time for his girlfriend or having fun with his friends anymore. When Jon thinks about his stress waves, he sees a huge tidal wave; he sees himself barely able to stay afloat!

* * *

Sabrina, on the other hand, finds balance between doing her homework, spending time with her friends, and going to dance classes. Sabrina finds that her waves are pretty small, and when they do come through, they are manageable. When her waves get too big, she takes it as a sign that she needs to change something in her schedule. When she does, her waves get smaller again.

Think for a minute about what is stressing you out right now. Imagine translating all of these stressors into the image of a wave. It might be a tidal wave or a very small wave; it is up to you.

In the rectangle provided below, draw a picture of what your *stress waves* look like right now.

Label these waves above with the stressors, worries, and/or fears that created them.

Describe your waves (for example, as big, small, mean, fierce, calm, mellow, or another description).

_____

_____

What thoughts come up for you when you look at the image you drew and the labels you added on the waves?

_____

_____

_____

What feelings come up for you when you look at this image and the labels on the waves?

_____

_____

something more

Grounding Anchor: Drop Your Anchor

To reduce your stress waves, imagine you are in a rowboat in the middle of the waves you just drew and you drop an anchor deep below the surface of the water. Even in the strongest of storms with huge crashing waves on the surface of the water, deep below the waves, the water is perfectly calm and still. This grounding anchor you drop from your boat to get to your calm and still waters can be your breath, your heartbeat, noticing the air around your fingers, your feet walking on the ground, or something else that grounds you. Use your grounding anchors when you are having a lot of "stress waves."

What grounding anchors do you have to help you drop down into the calm and still waters below your stress waves?

_____

_____

_____

_____

> mindful takeaway   Remember to use your grounding anchors—your breath, hands, heartbeat, or feet—when you feel that your stress waves are too big and you want to drop below into the calm, still waters below the surface.

Breathing is an automatic process. Like your heartbeat, it just happens, most often without your even noticing it.

Take a few seconds right now to notice your breathing. What was it like?

_____

_____

When Todd first noticed his breathing, he changed it and took really deep breaths, as if a doctor had put a stethoscope on his back and instructed him to take a deep breath.

Mindful Breathing Practice

Mindful breathing is noticing your breath as it is naturally occurring in the moment. When you begin to focus on your breath, it might change in some way, perhaps getting deeper or shallower.

If you notice that your breath has shifted, remind yourself that you can focus on your breath again just as it is. You don't need to take deep breaths.

Now for about thirty seconds to a minute, try to notice your breathing just as it is. Try to tune into the normal cadence and rhythm of your breath.

What did you notice when you did this?

_____

_____

What was your breathing like this time? Was it the same or different? Explain.

_____

_____

Mindful breathing can help you calm down or reduce your stress. When you check in with your breath on a regular basis, you notice what your breathing is like when it is "normal." As a counterpoint, you can notice what your breath is like when it isn't "normal," indicating that something is off emotionally or physically. Your breath can be a red flag providing you with information you can use to feel better by adjusting a situation. For example, if your breath is shallow, tight, or restricted, you might be experiencing fear, anxiety, or anger. Noticing this, you might be able to change the people you are with or the place or situation you are in.

mindful takeaway   If you are a visual person, imagine a picture of an anchor in your chest and think of your breath as an anchor to the present moment. This grounding anchor is always here with you when you notice it.

something more

Mindfully pay attention to your breath, body, and mind.

Notice your breath.

Pay attention to your nose and mouth. Which do you use to breathe in and out?

Notice your body while you breathe.

Notice your belly rise and fall. If you want to, place one or both of your hands on your stomach and feel the movement.

What did you notice as your breath flowed through your entire body?

_____

_____

_____

What was your breathing like when you paid attention to your body?

_____

_____

_____

Notice your mind while you breathe.

What thoughts and feelings did you notice as you breathed? For example, you might have noticed feeling angry or sad. You can say to yourself, *Breathing in, I calm my mind and body; breathing out, I release all I hold in my mind and body.*

_____

_____

_____

If you were distracted by thoughts, feelings, or discomforts, were you able to return to your breath? If so, how was that for you? And if you didn't find yourself distracted, what was that like?

_____

_____

_____

mindful takeaway   If you have difficulty focusing on your breath and get distracted, you can say to yourself, *Breathing in one, breathing out one, breathing in two, breathing out two.* Do this for a count of five. You can also count breaths at other times. For example, if you are walking into a tough class at school or about to have a hard conversation with a friend or family member, count your breaths.

paying attention to your mind: 21
sitting mindfulness practice

In this formal mindfulness practice, you notice your mind, body, and breath while sitting and not engaging in any other activity. This practice helps you tune into what it is like to be with partial silence, to be without so many electronic distractions. It helps you learn how to be comfortable without all the noises of everyday life.

During a practice, always feel free to readjust yourself to be more comfortable. If you ever feel the practice is harming you, go ahead and stop the practice altogether!

Sitting Mindfulness Practice

Total practice time: 5–10 minutes

You can reduce or add time to your sitting practice to fit your comfort level.

1. **Get comfortable and check in.** (This part takes a minute or two.)

   Find a place where you feel comfortable and safe, and where there are the fewest disruptions. Turn off electronics. Choose a comfortable seated position.

   What kind of day are you having? How could what has been happening in your day affect this sitting mindfulness practice? If you are very distracted and find it hard to sit right now, give yourself the time you need before you begin. Attend to what you need to, and then return to this practice.

   Gently close your eyes if you feel comfortable doing so.

   When you are ready, briefly scan your body. Notice any physical sensations you have. Bring your breath into any areas that have pain or discomfort. Breathe out any tension, pain, or discomfort.

Begin to feel the physical sensation of sitting. Notice how your body makes contact with the surface you are sitting on. Bring your awareness to the touch and pressure of this connection. Allow your body to relax into where you are sitting and settle into this moment.

Bring your attention to your stomach. Begin to notice how your belly moves as you breathe, how it rises on the in-breath and gently falls on the out-breath. If it helps you to notice your breath, you can place one or both of your hands on your belly and feel the motion. Without changing your breath, notice your breath as it moves through your entire body. Bring awareness to your nose and mouth, and notice where you bring air in and out: your nose or your mouth.

After completing this part, set a timer for the time you would like to do the sitting practice so you can close your eyes and don't have to focus on this book or the time.

2. **Be with your mind.** (This part is where the majority of time during your sitting practice will be spent.)

Sit and just notice what arises in your mind, both your thoughts and feelings.

When thoughts and feelings arise, just notice them. You don't have to do anything with them. Remember, you don't have to jump on the train of thoughts. You might say to yourself, *Oh, interesting; this is what I am thinking* (or feeling) *right now*, and guide your attention gently back to your breath and your body. You can also count breaths if that helps center you. Remember the anchor point you previously identified as helpful to you, and turn to it when needed.

Each time you get distracted noticing thoughts or feelings, remind yourself that it is normal; it is what your mind naturally does. Acknowledge that you got distracted and have come back to the practice. You are being mindful when you notice that you got distracted.

When you are finished with your practice, slowly move the tips of your fingers or toes and bring yourself back to your surroundings. You can choose to bring a piece of this moment and how you are feeling right now to the rest of your day.

Remember, there is no need to judge this sitting mindfulness practice as good or bad. Just accept it as time you spent for you to rest with what is.

something more

Debrief your sitting mindfulness practice.

What thoughts came to you?

_____

_____

_____

What feelings came up for you?

_____

_____

_____

How was it to sit and do nothing else?

_____

_____

_____

What was it like to be in partial silence and without electronics?

_____

_____

_____

If you got distracted, what distracted you? Were you able to bring yourself back?

_____

_____

_____

Did anything surprise you? If so, what was it?

_____

_____

_____

mindful takeaway   Whenever you do this practice, come to it with fresh eyes. Rather than judging how you did, know that it will be different each time you do it.

taking in the good: doing what you enjoy 22

There are probably days when you are so busy or upset that you don't take the time to do things you enjoy or enjoy the things you are doing that are pleasant to you. On the worst of days, you might even forget that there are things that bring you happiness, peace, or joy. Or perhaps you are doing these things, but not remembering to notice that they make you feel better.

> *Mira got into a fight with her parents this morning before school. Then she got her algebra test back and saw that she had flunked it. When she got her lunch, she dropped her tray on the floor, and everyone nearby turned to stare at her. She felt like her day was the worst ever!*

> *Brandon got a letter saying that he hadn't been accepted by the college he wanted to go to. He was very upset and also worried about telling his parents. He wanted to contact his friends for support, but he couldn't. On top of everything, he had been grounded for coming home late last weekend, and his social media privileges had been taken away.*

When you have had a bad day like Mira's or Brandon's, it is the perfect time to think of the things that bring a smile to your face or help you feel better, and do one or more of them. If you are down in the dumps, so to speak, you don't have to stay there; you can do something about it.

Read this list of activities (use the blanks lines to add any others), and put a check mark next to all the ones you enjoy doing. Then go back and put a star next to your top three.

- ☐ spending time with pets
- ☐ nature/being in the outdoors
- ☐ writing, journaling, blogging
- ☐ Internet, social networking, messaging, posting
- ☐ taking pictures
- ☐ doing a hobby or craft
- ☐ playing or listening to music
- ☐ spending time with your friends
- ☐ spending time with your family
- ☐ gardening
- ☐ drawing or painting
- ☐ exercising
- ☐ playing a sport
- ☐ mindfulness practice
- ☐ doing yoga
- ☐ reading
- ☐ taking a shower or bath

- ☐ watching movies
- ☐ volunteering
- ☐ eating out
- ☐ going to a sporting event
- ☐ going to a concert
- ☐ camping out
- ☐ traveling
- ☐ talking on the phone
- ☐ going to a mall or shopping
- ☐ dancing
- ☐ singing
- ☐ cooking
- ☐ building projects
- ☐ playing video games
- ☐ driving
- ☐ skiing or snowboarding
- ☐ other: _____
- ☐ other: _____

mindful takeaway   If you aren't feeling good, you can always turn to this list and do something to make yourself feel better. Download a copy of this list at http://www.newharbinger.com/40187 and complete it, take a picture of this page, or copy down the list of those activities you enjoy and put it somewhere you will see it often, for example, next to your bed, or on the mirror or fridge.

something more

You might think that you don't have time to do activities you like and enjoy. But no matter how busy you are, you can do things that are pleasant and don't take a lot of time; for example, noticing the sun or a pretty flower, enjoying the aroma and appearance of what you are about to eat, or appreciating a conversation with a friend. Learning to notice what little things in your life can bring you happiness—and focusing on them rather than on the negatives—will improve your mood and reduce your stress.

Write down the three activities you starred earlier. Then choose two more and add them.

1. _____

2. _____

3. _____

4. _____

5. _____

This week, do at least two of these activities. After you do each, reflect on what it was like to take the time to do something you enjoyed. Write about it here.

Activity 1: _____

_____

_____

_____

Activity 2: _____

_____

_____

_____

23 focusing on the positive: the pleasant moments calendar

Most people think they want to be happy and enjoy their lives, and many express that desire in words. But actually being happy and doing things you enjoy takes more work than just a passing thought or statement; it involves actively noticing and doing what makes you happy.

> *Olivia was really happy. She was going to get her braces off after two years, and she just found out that she got a B on her biology test, which had been really hard for her. When she left the class, she got a hug from her best friend.*

* * *

> *Tristan was excited because his parents had agreed to let him go to a battle of the bands show, where his favorite band would be playing.*

Many people allow one negative event to outweigh the positives of their day, but there are almost always good moments, even on days that might seem downright awful. You might not always notice these good moments if you are caught up in, or focused on, the negative. Like Olivia and Tristan, you can look for the good moments and pay attention to the things that make you happy.

Notice one pleasant moment every day for the next week and add it to the calendar that follows.

First, tell what the moment was. Then describe any thoughts or feelings you experienced before, during, and after the moment. Next, tell what you felt in your body before, during, and after the moment. Finally, tell how you feel and what you are thinking right now. You can download a copy of the calendar at http://www. newharbinger.com/40187.

> mindful takeaway   Instead of a day being all good or all bad, work on noticing a day just being what it is: a string of many moments, some pleasant or good, others unpleasant or bad. How could thinking this way change your perspective?

Pleasant Moments Calendar

	The Moment	My Thoughts and Feelings	What I Felt in My Body	What I Think and Feel Now
Example	I passed my driver's test.	I can't wait to drive to the lake! I was really excited.	I had butterflies in my stomach during the test. Afterward, I couldn't stop smiling and messaging my friends.	I hope my mom lets me borrow her car. I'm still really happy and can see how it is going to change so many things in my life.
Monday				
Tuesday				
Wednesday				

	The Moment	My Thoughts and Feelings	What I Felt in My Body	What I Think and Feel Now
Thursday				
Friday				
Saturday				
Sunday				

something more

Even though you've been working on your pleasant moments calendar, think about your day today. What was a moment that was unpleasant?

_____

_____

What thoughts led you to believe that this was an unpleasant moment?

_____

_____

What feelings led you to believe that this was an unpleasant moment?

_____

_____

Even though there was something unpleasant in your day, were you still able to notice what was pleasant?

_____

_____

mindful takeaway   When something unpleasant has occurred and you can still notice pleasant moments, you can shift from what is called *black-or-white* or *all-or-nothing* thinking and see that a day is made up of many moments—some pleasant and some unpleasant.

24 focusing on the negative: the unpleasant moments calendar

It is said that part of life is to take the bad with the good. People often want to push away or avoid bad times, but if you never have bad times, you might not be able to notice good times.

> At school, Rachel tripped in front of some people in the hallway. In her first class, her favorite teacher called her out for messaging in class. She got so upset that a few people laughed at her, which embarrassed her and made her even more upset. She then went to hand in her English essay and realized she had left it home.

Days like Rachel's will happen. Simply noticing when you are having a bad day without adding more emotion or thoughts to it will make it just a bad day and nothing more. Doing this will prevent a bad day from getting worse.

Notice one unpleasant moment every day for the next week and add it to this calendar.

First, tell what the moment was. Then describe any thoughts or feelings you experienced before, during, and after the moment. Tell what you felt in your body before, during, and after the moment. Finally, tell how you feel and what you are thinking right now. You can download a copy at http://www.newharbinger.com/40187.

Unpleasant Moments Calendar

	The Moment	My Thoughts and Feelings	What I Felt in My Body	What I Think and Feel Now
Example	My friend posted an embarrassing selfie of mine to the group we hang out with.	I thought that it would get spread around school and put on social media. I was worried that the rest of my friends would be mad at me. Afterward, I felt hurt and sad.	My face turned beet red. My chest got tight and I had a hard time breathing.	I am pissed off. I feel like I can't trust anyone— even my closest friends.
Monday				
Tuesday				
Wednesday				

The Moment	My Thoughts and Feelings	What I Felt in My Body	What I Think and Feel Now
Thursday			
Friday			
Saturday			
Sunday			

After your week is over, answer these questions:

What was your experience of looking for the negative? Did it make you feel worse or change your mood in some way?

_____

_____

_____

Which of these events resolved themselves pretty quickly?

_____

_____

_____

Which of these events is more chronic or longer-lasting?

_____

_____

_____

something more

Thinking about your day today, what is a moment that was pleasant (even though you are working on your unpleasant moments calendar)?

_____

_____

_____

What thoughts led you to believe that this was a pleasant moment?

_____

_____

_____

What feelings led you to believe that this was a pleasant moment?

_____

_____

_____

things you can and can't control 25

If you could control everything that happened in your life, there would be no reason to get stressed out because things would work out just the way you wanted them to. Unfortunately, no one has that much power, and the things that stress people out are often out of their control.

You undoubtedly realize you can't control certain things, like the weather, how much math homework you get, and what time you have to be at school. Then there are things you can't control, but perhaps think you can, like other people, places, things, or situations.

> Molly and Rebecca had talked about shopping together for clothes to go out in over the weekend. Molly was really looking forward to shopping with Rebecca, but every time she tried to settle on a day to go, Rebecca had something else to do. Molly decided to invite another friend to go with her.

No matter how much Molly wanted to shop with Rebecca, she could not control what Rebecca did. Once she realized that, she was able to change her own actions.

For each of these categories, list some problems you have recently had or are now having.

Family

_____

_____

_____

Relationships

_____

_____

School, work, or extracurricular activities

_____

_____

_____

Physical or mental health

_____

_____

_____

Behaviors to escape or avoid feelings (for example, risky sexual behavior, drug or alcohol use, or self-injury)

_____

_____

_____

Looking at your answers in the different categories, circle the problems you have some control over and are able to change. Cross out the ones you have no control over.

Focus your effort on the problems you have control over and can change.

mindful takeaway   Imagine that you are involved in a play, and instead of playing just the one character part you have been assigned, you try to control the entire play by being the director, all the actors, the set designer, the stage manager, and more. In real life, all you can control is yourself, your one part, and everyone else in the play is out of your control.

something more

Caring vs. Worrying

It is great to care about the people in your life, but there is a line between caring and worrying. As much as you might want to change the outcome of how things turn out for your friends or family, and no matter how much you worry, worrying will not change anything for others, or even for yourself.

You can listen to your friends, give them a shoulder to cry on, and be there for them, but don't let their problems consume your life. And when you have a problem of your own, don't keep it all inside; let your friends listen back.

List the things in your life, or friends' or family members' lives, that are worrying you right now.

_____

_____

_____

Of these, which can you affect or control by your worrying?

_____

This question is a trick one. You should have written nothing because you can't change anything by worrying. When you notice yourself worrying, you can remind yourself that it won't actually change the outcome or help solve or fix the problem—and might actually make things worse.

26 mindful stopping: responding instead of reacting

Have you ever acted impulsively and later wished you hadn't? *Mindful stopping* is a way for you to check in with yourself before you act impulsively or thoughtlessly in stressful moments. You can use this practice to respond to a situation instead of reacting to it.

> *One day at school, a girl calls Destiny a "fat whale" as they are about to pass each other in the hall. Destiny is so angry that she puts out her foot and trips the girl. She ends up in the principal's office.*

Mindful stopping could have helped Destiny from harming another, and herself, for that matter. Here's how it works.

Mindful Stopping Practice

1. Visualize a stop sign. You can also say to yourself, "Stop," in a firm but gentle voice.

2. Check in with your body. Begin with the tips of your toes and move up to the top of your head. Along the way, notice if anything is tight or tense, or just does not feel right.

3. Imagine bringing your breath into the places that feel discomfort. For example, you might have a tight feeling in your chest, your hands might feel tingly, and your stomach might hurt. Be aware of your body, and breathe in. If it helps, say to yourself, *Breathing in one, breathing out one, breathing in two, breathing out two*, for a few breaths until you feel less tense. You can also say to yourself, *Breathing in fresh air, breathing out discomfort.*

4. Take a breath. This time, imagine bringing in air through a small hole at the top of your head. Let the breath move from the top of your head through your body, and release it out through the tips of your toes.

Ask yourself these questions:

- How do I feel now?

- How do I want to respond?

- Do I want to respond to myself?

- Do I want to respond to someone else?

- Am I overreacting?

- Am I judging myself or others?

Ask yourself, *Do I need some time before I decide what I want to do?*

Taking some time will often let you see a situation more clearly. You might make a different choice, which might prevent a problem or avoid negative consequences.

mindful takeaway   The next time you are in a disagreement with a friend or family member, remember to take a mindful stop, allowing for a response instead of an impulsive reaction.

something more

Describe a stressful situation in which you reacted without stopping yourself. This situation can be based on a thought you had about yourself or on someone else's actions or words.

How did you react to this situation?

_____

_____

Now imagine yourself going through the mindful stopping process in the same situation.

Is your response different? If so, how?

_____

_____

How could you have responded instead?

_____

_____

being mindful of harmful judgments 27

"I am ugly." "I am fat." "I am stupid." "I'll never make the team." Do you ever find yourself having thoughts like these? If your answer is yes, you are listening to an inner voice of negative self-judgment.

Judgment involves assigning some value to situations, defining them as good or bad, right or wrong. It is a type of thought. Once a judgment persists long enough, it becomes a belief. Judgments can cause people to feel negative about themselves, others, and situations.

Helpful judgments

- allow you to process things quicker by using your memory;

- alert you to harm or danger;

- are based in fact or reality.

Harmful judgments

- are not based in fact or reality;

- are often based on your own beliefs or values, or those of others;

- are about performance, appearance, behaviors, actions, ability, age, speech, and worth.

Harmful judgments are not necessarily true. Just because you think a judgment, you don't have to believe it.

You can free yourself from a lot of added suffering, pain, and stress by learning to notice and free yourself from your negative inner critic without judging yourself.

What harmful judgments do you have about yourself?

_____

_____

_____

Harmful Judgment Journal Practice

Choose one of the harmful judgments you just wrote, and follow these steps to be mindful of it.

1. State and write the harmful judgment.

   Example: *I am ugly. I couldn't look good if I tried.*

   _____

   _____

2. Tell what makes it a harmful judgment.

   Example: *"I am ugly" is a judgment because it involves adding a value to how I look. There is no objective way to measure if I am ugly or not. Also, "I couldn't look good if I tried" is a judgment because "looking good" is in the eye of the beholder, and I couldn't possibly know if others would actually see me as looking good or not.*

   _____

   _____

   _____

3. With openness, gentleness, kindness, and curiosity, acknowledge what the judgment is and that it is a thought.

   Example: *Oh, interesting. The judgmental thought I am thinking right now is, "I am ugly."*

4. Notice whether this judgmental thought is unusual or if you have a pattern of judging yourself this way.

   Example: *I tend to say I am ugly a lot to myself and to my friends. They get at mad at me when I say it.*

5. When you think about this harmful judgment, how do you feel?

   Example: *I feel like crap. When one judgment pops up, usually more do, and I just start going on and on about all my so-called negative qualities. It's a cycle that really puts me in a bad mood and affects me all day.*

   _____

   _____

   _____

6. Think of what you could tell yourself instead.

   Example: *I am not feeling too great today. I don't think I look my best.*

   _____

   _____

   _____

After going through these six steps, what have you learned about your judgment?

Example: *This judgment wasn't helping me at all. I can just notice that I had the judgment, let it go, and move on. Being mindful allows me to right-size my negative thinking brain. It sometimes goes places I don't want it to, and I can notice this and move on.*

_____

_____

_____

Are there any key insights you have about being mindful of your harmful judgments? If so, share them here.

_____

_____

_____

mindful takeaway You are being mindful and aware when you notice a judgment and assess whether it is a harmful or helpful one.

something more

People don't make harmful judgments only about themselves. They also tend to judge others this way, including people who are close to them and people they don't like or even know.

What are some harmful judgments you have made about friends or family members?

_____

_____

_____

What are some harmful judgments you have made about people you don't like?

_____

_____

_____

What are some harmful judgments you have made about people you don't know?

_____

_____

_____

Do you think that judging others this way contributes to your stress? If so, tell how.

_____

_____

_____

mindful messaging and posting 28

Nowadays, life is often centered online. Most often, communicating with your friends is not face-to-face but through messages and posts. Mistakes and misunderstandings can happen when you have to rely on someone else's ability to interpret what you wrote or, in reverse, on interpreting what others have written.

> *Sue is chatting with her friends on WhatsApp, watching E!, and posting on Instagram all at the same time. Suddenly, she realizes that she posted her pic for her private feed to her public feed, and she is freaking out because it can't be undone. She's worried about who's going to see this pic, take a screenshot of it, and send it out to everyone. She doesn't know what to do and starts having a panic attack.*

Think about some of the snafus that have happened to you in the virtual world or that you have heard about at your school. Here are some things people tell me over and over that they wish they hadn't done online:

- sent a message to the wrong person

- sent a message before it was done

- posted a picture or video they wish they hadn't

Most of the day, you are texting, posting, or engaging in some other type of messaging. How often are you thoughtful about what you write, post, or share? *Mindful messaging and posting* is about being thoughtful about what you write, post, or share in the online world.

It can help prevent the following:

- regrettable and embarrassing situations;

- someone from getting mad at you;

- you from sending the wrong things;

- you getting into trouble;

- hurting other people;

- doing something you can't undo.

Mindful Messaging and Posting Practice

There are four steps to mindful messaging and posting:

1. Reread what you have written before you hit send or post.

2. Pause for a second or two before you hit send or post to make sure you want to.

3. Ask yourself if the message you are going to send has been thought out, is not rushed, and has a purpose.

4. Check in with how you are feeling emotionally and physically right now. What emotions are you having? What red flags, signals, or cues is your body giving off?

   Note: If you are feeling jealous, angry, frustrated, sad, or depressed, or experiencing any other negative emotion, consider pausing and *not* messaging or posting right now.

By following these steps, you can avoid a lot of messaging and posting regrets.

Look at a few of the messages and posts you wrote over the last day or two.

Is there anything you sent that you wish you hadn't?

_____

_____

What, if anything, about them would you like to change?

_____

_____

Rereading these, are there one or two you can think of a way to write more thoughtfully? Write them here:

_____

_____

_____

_____

mindful takeaway   The next time you create a message or post, do so mindfully. Remember: reread, pause for a few seconds, consider the purpose of the message, notice your feelings, and choose to PAUSE or hit SEND.

something more

Take the time today to call a friend on the phone instead of messaging or posting.

Who did you call?

_____

What did you talk about?

_____

_____

How was it different from just messaging or posting?

_____

_____

mindful takeaway   Ask yourself sometimes, *Would it be more meaningful if I called my friend instead of sending a message or post?* If the answer is yes, pick up the phone.

playing out the end of the movie 29

When you are trying to make a decision, it can help to play out the movie. Ask yourself, *If this situation were a movie, how would it end?* What consequences would your actions lead to?

Think of a time when you made a choice and didn't like the way the "movie" ended.

Describe the situation.

_____

_____

_____

_____

If you had played out the movie beforehand, what would you have done differently?

_____

_____

_____

_____

something more

You can't change the past, but you can learn from your mistakes. Think of a situation in your life that you are trying to decide on now. Describe it here.

_____

_____

_____

_____

What choices do you have in this situation?

_____

_____

_____

How would the movie play out with each choice?

_____

_____

_____

_____

_____

_____

life events can cause stress

Sad or tragic events can obviously be stressful. But all kinds of things can cause stress—even events you might think of as positive, such as getting your driver's license or getting into the college you wanted to. Any change in your life—good or bad—has the potential to be stressful to you.

On the chart that follows, the events have been grouped according to the level of stress they are likely to generate for most people. Any single event might be more or less stressful for you, and that's okay. Feel free to shift any event to a different category if you consider it to be more or less stressful.

Circle all the events you have experienced within the last six months. If there are events in your life that aren't listed, you can write them on the blank lines.

Now figure out your score for each of the categories.

Number of highly stressful events you circled x 20 = _____

Number of moderately stressful events you circled x 10 = _____

Number of somewhat stressful events you circled x 5 = _____

Add these three scores to get your total score: _____

Which range do you fall into? Circle it below.

0–20: There are not too many stressful events in your life.

21–80: Your stress level might cause you problems mentally or physically.

81–100: Stress is most likely affecting your life negatively.

101 and up: You are probably experiencing many stress-related problems in your life.

Highly Stressful	Moderately Stressful
Death of a family member	Change in which parent you live with
Death of a friend	Trying to please your parent(s) or live up to their expectations
Divorce or separation of parents	Change in personal or family financial status
Loss of a pet	Change in number of arguments with your parent(s)
Abuse (sexual, physical, or mental)	
Problems with the legal system	Trouble with your parent(s) or sibling(s)
Illness (physical or mental)	Being expelled or suspended from school
Change of health in someone close to you	Having a new stepparent or stepsibling
Pregnancy or abortion	Being bullied
Sexuality issues	Loss of a best friend
Use of drugs, alcohol, sex, or self-injury	Switching schools
Other: _____	Moving
Other: _____	Other:_____
	Other:_____

Somewhat Stressful	
Public humiliation	Getting into college
Earning more money than before	Change in sleeping habits
Having a false rumor spread about you	Friend moving
Change in time spent on technology	Trouble with teacher(s)
Change in friendships	Taking SATs, school achievement tests, or Advanced Placement tests
Change in number of arguments with friend(s)	Getting a bad grade
Change in responsibilities at home	High school graduation
Getting a driver's license	Increased workload at school
Public speaking	Taking an Advanced Placement class
Getting grounded or losing privileges	Grades worse than expected
Applying to college	Trying out for an activity
Achieving or accomplishing something new	Getting on a sports team, cheerleading squad, play, or musical
	Other: _____
	Other:_____

something more

Whatever your score, it is not meant to make you feel worse or stress you out more, but it can help you be aware of what you are facing that may be impacting your physical and mental health.

Which of the events you circled are causing you the most stress?

_____

_____

Which, if any, of these events are in the process of ending?

_____

_____

Which of these events are out of your control?

_____

_____

Which events could you work on changing to decrease your stress level?

_____

_____

What did you learn about yourself by doing this exercise?

_____

_____

You might want to do this activity again in the future to see if your stress level has changed.

coping with painful events 31

At one time or another, everyone experiences painful or upsetting events. Painful events like doing poorly in a class, getting fired from a job, not getting into the college you wanted to, or losing a friend are all problems that can naturally cause suffering, emotional or physical pain, and stress.

How you choose to respond to and cope with painful life problems affects your overall level of stress, as well as your ability to manage problems. Often people add to their pain and stress by *blocking* it, which will make a stressful situation even worse.

Blocking a problem can include any of these:

- engaging in unhelpful or harmful coping behaviors

- resisting the problem

- avoiding the problem

- pushing the problem away

- denying that the problem exists

- ignoring the pain it causes

- feeling guilty about it

- obsessing about it

- ruminating about it

- judging yourself

- telling yourself that you should have done something differently

It may be helpful to have this list to print out and post. Download it from http://www.newharbinger.com/40187.

Do you find that you try to cope or manage any of your problems with these blocking behaviors? If so, which of these do you use?

_____

_____

Does using these blocking behavior(s) actually help you solve, cope with, or manage your problem, or make it worse? If so, how?

_____

_____

Amir's girlfriend, Emma, broke up with him a few weeks ago after she hooked up with his best friend. He is still messaging her at least ten times a day, checking her relationship status, and bugging her friends about what she is doing. He has stopped going out with his friends and started to skip basketball practice, and he is staying up online until four in the morning. He can't stop thinking about Emma.

Amir is obviously going to feel some pain, but he can reduce his stress and how much pain he feels by changing his blocking actions. Thinking this out, he sees that he needs and wants to stop doing these things, as they are just making him feel worse. He can choose to spend time with his friends who will help him feel better. He can put his phone away at night so he doesn't feel like such a zombie at school. When he sees Emma at school, he can remind himself that it will take time to get over the breakup.

The first step to coping with and managing a problem in a healthy way is to notice what you are doing that is blocking. The second step is to stop doing that which is hurting you, not helping you.

Tell about a problem in your life right now that is causing you suffering, pain, and stress.

_____

_____

What blocking behaviors are you engaging in?

_____

_____

Of those things, are any making your situation better?

_____

_____

Of those things, are any making your situation worse?

_____

_____

Which blocking behaviors can you change or stop doing?

_____

_____

mindful takeaway   If what you're doing isn't working, you can do something different!

something more

In the future, when you encounter a painful problem, ask yourself what you are doing to try to cope with and manage it. Go over the list of blocking behaviors and notice which, if any, you are engaging in. Think about what you can do to change, reduce, or even eliminate the blocking behavior(s) you are engaging in.

Consider the stress you feel in connection with the situation above.

How do you feel now?

_____

_____

What are you going to do now that you have given this problem some thought?

_____

_____

mindful takeaway   You have the control and power to decide how you want to respond to life problems instead of automatically reacting to them.

unhelpful and harmful coping behaviors 32

Not all ways people cope with stress are helpful. Some people engage in coping behaviors that are unhelpful, or even harmful, perhaps thinking that these behaviors will somehow fix their problems. Instead, they often find that the behavior doesn't fix these problems, which may even get worse, and can even cause further problems.

Jessica was fighting with her parents over her being on her phone too much and staying up too late. She was sick of the fighting and decided that when her parents were asleep she would sneak out. She used her parents' credit card number to order a ride to go to this guy's house. He went to another local high school, and she didn't know him very well. She went there just to get to know him better and hang out, but ended up sleeping with him. It was her first time. She went home thinking they were going to have an ongoing relationship. He texted her the next day saying he wasn't interested, and he never communicated with her again. Later that month when her parents got the bill, she was grounded for sneaking out and using their credit card.

✳ ✳ ✳

A year ago, Anthony started taking pills at parties with his friends. He felt like the pills made him funnier and helped him fit in. After a while, he found he needed to use just to get through the day. It wasn't long before he began to steal prescription pills from his parents. Anthony's problems went from bad to worse one night when his girlfriend, Laurie, slumped over unconscious. She had OD'd on the pills they had been taking together. Medical responders were able to revive Laurie, and her parents enrolled her in a wilderness program where she worked on her mental health. Anthony was cut from any and all sports and extracurricular activities through the end of the school year. He was mandated to attend a substance abuse treatment program.

Many unhelpful and harmful coping behaviors can get out of control and become life threatening—sometimes very quickly! What started for Anthony as a way, he thought, to have fun became a harmful addiction that led to serious consequences for him and Laurie.

Put a check mark next to any of these coping behaviors you have engaged in during the past year. If you prefer to note the behaviors in your mind rather than checking them, that's okay.

☐ alcohol use

☐ sexting

☐ posting pictures of you doing something that can be harmful to you or others

☐ drug use, including improper use of prescription drugs

☐ smoking cigarettes

☐ isolating yourself

☐ having unprotected sex

☐ having multiple sex partners

☐ cutting yourself

☐ burning your body

☐ bullying

☐ getting into illegal activities

☐ binge eating

☐ making yourself vomit after eating

☐ excessive exercising

☐ stealing

☐ associating with people you know aren't good for you

☐ getting into fights

☐ hoarding

If you are engaging in any of the above behaviors, take a hard look at the positive and negative outcomes you are getting as a result. Honesty is key! Please list those outcomes here:

Behavior	Negative Outcomes	Positive Outcomes
Example: *I cut myself when my parents yelled at me about my GPA.*	*Feel numb* *Denial* *Can permanently scar* *Hurts me both physically and mentally* *Issue is still there* *Feel a sense of shame*	*Temporarily eases my feelings* *People pay more attention to me*

People often notice that the number of negative outcomes will greatly outweigh the positive outcomes. If you listed any positive outcomes, go back and look at them. Are they really positive outcomes? Are they actually making your problem better in any way?

If you listed any negative outcomes, consider how engaging in these behavior(s) is actually harming or hurting you in some way. Write down your thoughts here:

_____

_____

_____

Sharing your concerns with others can help. Having someone to turn to when you aren't doing well is really important, whether it is a friend, a parent or other relative, or an adult at school or in the community. If you aren't comfortable sharing a particular problem with people like these, or you have a problem that seems too big for someone currently in your life to help with, consider speaking with a mental health professional.

mindful takeaway   Engaging in unhelpful coping behaviors might appear to put a Band-Aid on a problem—to push it away or numb it for a time—but the truth is that the original problem doesn't go away.

something more

Courage to Change

You can apply these often quoted words to any life problem that comes your way. They won't necessarily fix it or change it but can really help provide you with some valuable insight!

*"Give me the **strength** to accept the things I cannot change,*

*The **courage** to change the things I can and*

*The **wisdom** to know the difference!"*

When you think about these words, what comes up for you?

_____

_____

_____

Think of a problem in your life right now. Ask yourself these questions, and write down your answers.

What is the problem?

_____

_____

_____

If this problem is something you can change, what actual steps or things can you do to make a change?

_____

_____

_____

If this problem is something you can't change, can you accept that it is out of your control?

_____

_____

_____

When you think about yourself and strength, what comes up for you?

_____

_____

_____

When you think about yourself and courage, what comes up for you?

_____

_____

_____

When you think about yourself and wisdom, what comes up for you?

_____

_____

_____

What mindfulness practices can help you deal with difficult situations in your life?

_____

_____

_____

33 using self-care to manage problems

Taking good care of yourself through engaging in positive self-care behaviors is a healthy way to manage difficult life problems, instead of using unhelpful and harmful coping behaviors.

Here are some positive self-care behaviors. (Download this list, if you like, at http://www.newharbinger.com/40187.)

- Practice the mindfulness exercises you have been learning in this book.

- Set realistic goals for yourself.

- Say kind things to yourself.

- Eat healthy foods.

- Get enough sleep.

- Exercise.

- Notice positive thoughts and give less attention to negative ones.

- Have compassion for yourself.

- Ask for help when you need it.

- Turn off technology when it is negatively impacting your life.

- Do something that makes you smile.

- Listen to your favorite (cheerful) song.

- Spend time with people in your life who build you up, for example, friends or family members.

- Do something you love that would be considered healthy, even if it is just for a minute or two.

- Look at or be in nature.

These behaviors boost positive feelings. They can be used anytime, and they are especially helpful when you want to engage in an unhelpful or harmful coping behavior, or when you are feeling down, depressed, tired, isolated, or alone, or experiencing some other negative feeling.

When you engage in self-care, you are letting yourself know that you matter. When you read this sentence, what thoughts or feelings come up?

_____

_____

_____

What do you do right now to take care of yourself that might be considered good self-care?

_____

_____

What self-care behaviors would you like to do that you currently aren't?

_____

_____

_____

Start with one a day! Or even one a week.

Imagine your heart looks like this symbolic one. Using these questions as guidelines, fill in this outline:

Is your heart full or empty?

What self-care activities can you do to fill up your heart?

What colors does your heart have?

What thoughts or feelings are present in your heart?

If you find that your heart isn't the way you would like it to be, you may need to do more for yourself. And if your heart is to your liking, you can still add in an extra dose of self-care! (For a downloadable copy of the heart, visit http://www.newharbinger.com/40187)

something more

Self-Care vs. Being Selfish

Self-care is different from being selfish. Selfish people think only of themselves and aren't concerned about others. When you take care of your heart, mind, and body, you are not being selfish; you are helping yourself function well and be balanced in daily life. By taking care of yourself, you are making it possible to be there for yourself and others.

How do you define being selfish?

_____

_____

_____

How do you define self-care?

_____

_____

_____

It isn't selfish to let someone be there for you. Remember how it feels when you can be there for someone else.

When you think about whether you are or aren't a selfish person, what comes up for you?

_____

_____

_____

How can you ask for support or let others, like your friends or family members, be there for you?

_____

_____

_____

Are you always the friend who is there for someone else?

_____

_____

_____

mindful takeaway   Whenever you feel that taking care of yourself or making time for yourself is selfish, think twice. Remember this: The heart pumps blood to itself first before the other organs of the body. Similarly, you need to consider yourself before you can truly help or give to others. If you are giving to others when your virtual tank or bank is empty, you aren't going to be of much service.

tracking harmful behaviors: 34
the self-awareness calendar

Self-harm is about numbing and masking emotional pain by hurting yourself in some other, often very destructive, way. Self-harming behaviors act as temporary Band-Aids or distractions. When you want to engage in a harmful behavior like cutting, binging or purging, or using drugs or alcohol, tracking the behavior on a calendar before you actually do it can really help.

Filling out this self-awareness calendar can help you with three very important things:

- It can provide you with some information about and possible reason(s) why you want to hurt yourself.

- You can give yourself the time to think and reflect. You might decide not to hurt yourself.

- You can start to become aware of the people, places, things, or situations that are often the reason or cause for your wanting to harm yourself.

Follow these steps to complete the self-awareness calendar:

1. Identify the harmful behavior you want to do, and write it down.

2. Reflect on what was going on in your life right before you wanted to hurt yourself, and write it down.

3. Write down what you are thinking right now.

4. Write down what you are feeling right now.

5. PAUSE and take a mindful minute before you engage in the behavior. Just check in with your breath, your body, and your mind, including your thoughts and feelings.

6. Write down what you want to do now.

7. Visit http://www.newharbinger.com/40187 to download a calendar and for a bonus activity, the "Self-Harm Awareness Journal," on this topic.

Self-Awareness Calendar

	Harmful Behavior	What Happened Right Before	My Thoughts	My Feelings	After Pausing, What I Want to Do Now
Example 1	*I want to cut myself.*	*I flunked my test.*	*I am stupid.*	*I feel worthless.*	*I know cutting will not change what happened. I can see if I can retake my test. I can also study differently next time. I am still upset, but this feeling will pass.*
Example 2	*I want to vomit.*	*Someone mentioned I have a double chin.*	*I am fat, and no one is going to want to date me.*	*I feel alone.*	*I don't have to believe what I was told. I have friends and that is really important to me. I can go and do something positive for myself, like playing a game online with my friends.*

Self-Awareness Calendar

	Harmful Behavior	What Happened Right Before	My Thoughts	My Feelings	After Pausing, What I Want to Do Now
Time 1					
Time 2					
Time 3					
Time 4					
Time 5					

Before you harm yourself: 1. complete the calendar, 2. read, 3. pause, and 4. consider not hurting yourself.

What did you observe or learn?

_____

_____

_____

Did you notice any patterns around people, places, things, or situations that led you to want to harm yourself?

_____

_____

_____

Think about whether you still want to harm yourself.

Ask yourself if the situation that led you to want to hurt yourself in the first place would change if you engaged in the harming behavior.

Remember, your first thought to do something can often be wrong. Take a minute before you hurt yourself. You are not alone. You can do something different!

mindful takeaway   Remember that you don't have to engage in a harmful behavior just because you think about it or it comes to your mind. If you still want to harm yourself, please talk to an adult you trust: a professional, teacher, coach, mentor, or family member.

something more

Ice Cube Activity

When you find yourself about to engage in a self-harming behavior, try grabbing an ice cube and holding it in your hand until it melts completely. You might also try counting your breaths (breathing in one, breathing out one, breathing in two, breathing out two) while the ice cube melts.

Holding an ice cube will not make you feel emotionally worse after you do it, and it will not add to your problems. It can replace what you are trying to get by doing a self-harming behavior: distraction, numbing, and feeling something physically painful instead of feeling an emotional pain.

Try this activity now even if you aren't engaging in any harmful coping behavior.

What was that experience like?

_____

_____

When might you want to try it in the future?

_____

_____

mindful takeaway   Consider teaching a friend or two about grabbing an ice cube. It could help them when they aren't doing well.

35 next steps

Well done! Kudos! Congratulations! You have been on a journey of learning, growth, and self-discovery.

Go to the first activity in this book and look at the problems you wrote down. Which, if any, of these problems have ended or been resolved? List them here:

_____

_____

_____

Which, if any, of these problems are out of your control? List them here:

_____

_____

_____

Consider the idea and action of letting go of the problems that are out of your control. Spending your time on them will not change their outcome.

Of the problems you first wrote down, which remain active? List them in the problem column on the chart that follows. What new problems are currently in your life? List them in the problem column.

Under possible mindfulness-based solutions, write down any of the specific mindfulness-based activities, skills, or tools you've started using or plan to use to help with the problems you wrote down.

You can download a copy of this chart at http://www.newharbinger.com/40187.

Problem	Possible Mindfulness-Based Solutions
Example: *My parents are stressing me out.*	*Dropping-in mindfulness practice* *Mindful stopping* *Pleasant activities: do something I enjoy and that makes me happy*
Example: *I stay online so late that I am exhausted all day.*	*Put myself on a good sleep and computer hygiene schedule and routine* *Try doing the body scan mindfulness practice before I go to sleep* *Remember to use mindful messaging and posting tips when I am online*

Problem	Possible Mindfulness-Based Solutions

Take a picture of this chart or copy down what you have written above, and put it (or a copy of your downloaded chart) somewhere you will see it often, for example, next to your bed or on the mirror or fridge.

Periodically review and update what you wrote, removing problems that have resolved and including new problems that arise. Consider all the different tools in this book that you can use as possible mindfulness-based solutions to work on future problems that come your way.

Mindful Practice Reminders

Now that you have completed the activities in this book, you might be wondering about what to do next. The best way to continue to manage your stress and to grow and change is to spend time on the mindfulness practices you have learned.

When you pay attention to any of your senses no matter what you are doing, you are being mindful. As you engage in routine activities or interests, focusing in on any of your senses is another easy and accessible way to be mindful. You can use *informal* mindfulness practice—bringing mindful awareness to everything you already do in your life—so you don't have to spend any extra time.

When you have more time, you can do some of the more *formal* mindfulness practices you have learned, for example:

- Dropping-In Mindfulness Practice (activity 11)

- Mindful Eating Practice (activity 12)

- The Body Scan Mindfulness Practice (activity 13)

- Bringing Mindfulness to Walking and Movement (activity 14)

- Doing Homework or Taking a Test Mindfully (activity 15)

- Paying Attention to Your Breath (activity 20)

- Paying Attention to Your Mind: Sitting Mindfulness Practice (activity 21)

- Mindful Stopping: Responding Instead of Reacting (activity 26)

- Mindful Messaging and Posting (activty 25)

mindful takeaway   It is a good practice to get into the habit of checking in with your life and assessing whether you are where you want to be. You can create new problem lists and consider what skills you have learned that you would like to use to help you.

something more

To continue on your journey, take a sheet of paper and write a letter to yourself sharing where you are at this very moment in your life. Include what you want to remember from this book and what activities you want to keep doing as you move forward. Once you have written this letter, seal it in an envelope, and date it for three months from now.

After three months have passed, open your letter. You can set a reminder on your phone if it helps. When you reread it, reflect on where you are now. If you aren't doing what you wanted to be doing, you can start now. You might want to add to your original thoughts or change things based on your current life. Know that you can always write a letter to yourself to check in and keep reminding you of things in your life that you want to remember.

mindful takeaway   Remember that each day is a new and fresh day. Start anew.

acknowledgments

I believe teens are diamonds in the rough covered in coal. It is the job of the adults in teens' lives to help them uncover the beautiful shining diamonds they already are. I wish to thank all my clients and their parents, who have allowed me to grow as a therapist and create new and inventive ways to teach mindfulness. Not only do I get to teach teens and their families, I get the opportunity to learn from everyone I teach.

I wish to thank the mentors I have who share their wisdom and have made me the person I am today. Thanks to Rick Hanson, Dan Siegel, Jon Kabat-Zinn, Laurie Grossman, Lee Freedman, and Donna DiGiorgio.

I want to thank my mindful family and community of colleagues, friends, and professional students that fill my life, including, but not limited to, Todd Corbin, Marina Boliaris, Ana Floriani-O'Sullivan, Kerri Mahoney, Priscilla Taylor-Williams, Laurie Angress, Susan Kaiser-Greenland, Daniel Rechtschaffen, Jennifer Cohen-Harper, Theo Koffler, Heidi Bornstein, Chris Willard, and Whitney Stewart.

It is with the support of my mindful family, friends, and mentors that I live a blessed life. To my partner and soul mate, Steve Brashear, I am so grateful for your support, wisdom, and insight. Also, to my furry family—Bravest, Zoe, Squeaks, and Handsome: You are my children and fill my life with love and happiness every day.

Gina M. Biegel, LMFT, is a psychotherapist, researcher, speaker, and author in the San Francisco Bay Area who specializes in mindfulness-based work with adolescents. She is founder of Stressed Teens, which has been offering mindfulness-based stress reduction for teens (MBSR-T) to adolescents, families, schools, professionals, and the community for over a decade. She created MBSR-T to help teens in a large HMO's outpatient department of child and adolescent psychiatry who were not receiving relief or amelioration of their physical and psychological symptoms with the use of a multitude of other evidence-based practices. She is an expert and pioneer in bringing mindfulness-based approaches to youth. She is author of *Be Mindful Card Deck for Teens*. She also has a mindfulness practice audio CD, *Mindfulness for Teens*, to complement the MBSR-T program. She provides worldwide, intensive ten-week online trainings, and works with teens and families individually and in groups. Her work has been featured on *CNN*, *Reuters*, and in *The New York Times*. For more information, visit her website at www.stressedteens.com.